Against the Written Word

T0046939

Acknowledgments/thank you to Johnny Temple, Guy Picciotto, Rich Morel, Frances Stark, Tim Svenonius, Alexandra Cabral, Michelle Mae, and Experimental Jetset, for production assistance, help, and guidance. Made with the cooperation of the Alphabet Reform Committee.

Published by Akashic Books
©2023 Ian F. Svenonius

ISBN: 978-1-63614-080-3
Library of Congress Control Number: 2022933232
First printing

Cover design courtesy of Alexandra Cabral
Letterpress on cover by T. Svenonius
Illustrations by I.F. Svenonius
Author photograph opposite courtesy of Michelle Mae
Horse courtesy of Clif Taylor and Tasha Bundy
Author photograph on page 308 courtesy of Alexandra Cabral
"Babylon" graphic in Part IV by Experimental Jetset
Interior layout by Sohrab Habibion and Aaron Petrovich

Some of the content of this book has been presented or published before: "I Survived Reeducation Camp" was originally presented as a workshop at a Southern California music festival; "I Remember . . . Frankenstein" was produced as a play at the Hammer Museum in Los Angeles; "S.T.E.M." was presented as an electric lecture and light show at the Whitney Museum in New York; and "Manifesto of the People's Provisional Army for Alphabet Reform" was published as a part of I.F. Svenonius and the Experimental Jetset Group's Alphabet Reform Committee Headquarters installation at the Volksbühne on Rosa-Luxemburg-Platz, Berlin. Earlier versions of some essays were also featured in the *Cellophane Flag* periodical (Radical Elite Press).

Akashic Books
Brooklyn, New York
info@akashicbooks.com
akashicbooks.com

I.F. Svenonius

AUTHOR'S NOTE

The owner of this book is in no way responsible for its incendiary and out-of-control content. It was merely a gift which they, out of politeness, felt they could not refuse, and they only keep it out of a sense of obligation or maybe some perverse, unwholesome fascination.

Signed,
The Author

A NOTE ON THE
COVER DESIGN

You may have noticed that this book is slightly damaged, either from a fingerprint, a tiny smudge, a dinged corner, or some combination thereof.

Such blemishes, though normally grounds for exchanging a book, are actually an integral—and intentional—design aspect of *Against the Written Word*, the antiliteracy tract you're holding in your hands.

Against the Written Word ushers in an exciting new world of illiteracy, enforced by antiliterates dedicated to animalism. In this world, the tactile will be made paramount again; messages will no longer consist of letters, texts, or graffiti, but smudges, scuffs, and smells, which people will leave as markings to one another.

This copy of *Against the Written Word* may have been thumbed through already, by some curious thrill seeker, an on-the-run desperado, or even a potential lover. The preliterate signals they left on this book—whether they be smells, smudges, or crumpled corners—could be useful to you in locating a like-minded community in the postliterate era we are embarking on.

Therefore, while these sorts of irregularities would normally induce dissatisfaction and warrant a "return," in this particular case they are a vital component of the book; possibly its most salient feature. In fact, if this book isn't slightly marred or disfigured, exchange it for one that is.

Sincerely,
The Committee for Alphabet Reform

Against the Written Word

the

Written

Word

Toward a Universal Illiteracy

Ian F. Svenonius

AKASHIC BOOKS

Dedicated to the barbarians,
who are unable to read this book

DISCLAIMER BY BOOK OWNER

I, the owner of this book—Against the Written Word: Toward a Universal Illiteracy—*am in no way responsible for its content, and in no manner do I necessarily subscribe to its wild conceits.*

In fact, I only keep it around because I've been too lazy to dispose of it, or maybe I haven't gotten around to looking at it.

In the latter scenario, I don't even know what it is or how it got here.

Or perhaps I thought it was a bit of fluff; some sort of satirical text to be read aloud to one's lover at bedtime or for amusement at a party. If this book is found dog-eared on my bedside table or thumbed through next to my beach blanket, then someone may have planted it there to incriminate me.

Finally, if someone who resembles me has been seen passing out copies of Against the Written Word *to their colleagues and acquaintances, I'm not sure who that is; maybe a distant cousin or look-alike.*

Signed,

_____

Owner, this copy of *AGAINST THE WRITTEN WORD*

CONTENTS

PART III: THE EROTIC LIVES OF MACHINES

PART IV: ALPHABET REFORM

PREFACE

Wow! People really love this book you're holding in your hands.

They are going nuts for it. It's a kind of mass hysteria, with cuckoo reactions and accolades from those people known to be "in the know." Yes, normally reticent individuals are "heaping" it with hallelujahs. They are "burying" it in praise. It's kind of a trip. Let's listen in:

Critical Praise for
AGAINST THE WRITTEN WORD:
TOWARD A UNIVERSAL ILLITERACY
by I.F. Svenonius

"Finally, a book that will put an end to reading, writing, and arithmetic."
—Caspar Hasbin

"This book shows us that the *written* word is the *rotten* word—a trick, a ploy, a device to oppress."

—Guy de Boardwalk

"I will tell you what I think about this book 'in person' instead of 'in writing' because 'writing,' my dear, is just more of the same cynical propaganda."

—Eleanor Klutz

"This is a book which will solve mankind's condition of alienation, by going to the root of the matter: literacy itself. After the systems of alphabets and reading are smashed, then we shall confront the other foul systems that plague mankind. All hierarchies will be overturned. The sun will rise instead of fall. The moon will come out in the day. Babies will raise their parents, and food will taste people."

—Penelope Pittstop

"The alphabet is dead! We are now liberated from books and reading forever!! Watch out, math; numbers are next!!!"

—Frogman Mo

"Hallelujah! With this book comes liberation. Liberation from: the alphabet, books, magazines, ad copy, billboards, T-shirts with words on them, social media, manifestos, screeds, broadsheets, liner notes, acknowledgments, back-cover blurbs, fortune cookies, daily horoscopes, draft notices, passed notes in class, subtitles, librettos, essays, op-ed columns, PSAs on the sides of buses, government travel advisories, gift cards, bathroom-stall graffiti, pamphlets, text messages, ancient manuscripts, tomes, slogans scrawled in blood on the wall, sanctimonious running-dog journalists who are bootlicks to warmongering newspapers owned and operated by the military-industrial complex, and all the other deranged propaganda utilized against us by the ruling class. This is *the book to end all books*, vital to the next stage of human development. We relinquish reading gladly, just as mankind once relinquished serfdom and human sacrifice. *Against the Written Word* is a milestone achievement, and its author a *Great Liberator.*"

—Chairman Annie

A NOTE REGARDING
CRITICAL PRAISE

A book such as this one*, profound, singular, and flashing with brilliance, is typically celebrated by its partisans, who "heap it with praise."

This praise, though the intentions behind it may be good, can sometimes be laid on so thick that it actually serves to obscure the book itself. Such unregulated praise can bury and smother its subject, to the point where it can no longer really be "seen." The critical hyperbole and sensation becomes a kind of tomb, and the book (or piece of art, record, film, what have you) becomes encrypted; a mummy, remote and legendary.

Many works which are so entombed are reduced to a kind of caricature, and their content simplified for easy dinner-table banter. They become a kind of emblem, footnote, or hieroglyph to

---

* *Though, one could argue, there has never actually been a book quite like this.*

be tossed around in casual conversation, without regard to their actual message, essence, or "being."

This book, *Against the Written Word: Toward a Universal Illiteracy,* is too important for this obfuscating process of lazy mystification to be visited upon it. Therefore, while we appreciate the fanatic expressions of hyperbole—by influential persons of note and ho-hum bums alike—as well-meaning, entertaining, and earnest, we must regulate it so that it doesn't become an obstacle to understanding. All praise for this book must therefore be submitted to the committee for review before being allowed to join the deafening chorus of acclamation it already enjoys.

Once properly certified, this praise can be allowed to join the other foam-mouthed voices fanatically ballyhooing *Against the Written Word*, and together commence on a collective mission to cleanse the world, once and for all, of those confounded ABCs.

PART I

AGAINST THE WRITTEN WORD

"Yes, yes, if you please, no reference to examples in books. Men have every advantage of us in telling their own story. Education has been theirs in so much higher a degree; the pen has been in their hands. I will not allow books to prove any thing."
—Jane Austen, *Persuasion* (1817)

Against the Written Word

1

AGAINST THE WRITTEN WORD

Toward a Universal Illiteracy

I. THE BOOK TO END ALL BOOKS

This is the last book you will ever read.

In fact, after this book you will never feel the need to read anything, ever again.

Chances are, you will dedicate yourself to a new, unlettered life of sublime illiteracy and live out your days as an analphabetic ignoramus. Because this book will turn you *off* the written word—permanently.

Once you read this book, manifesto, screed, polemic—these distinctions will no longer matter in the future as all will be relics of the past—you will be hep to the innate corruption of the written word, its deceitful nature, and why the written versions of words differ so fundamentally from their spoken cousins (i.e., words used in person between people).

This book will furthermore reveal why literacy is the pet project of the ruling class. Why its institutionalization has been advanced so relentlessly and with such single-minded zeal, by an elite who are otherwise disinterested in public health and human rights. And, finally, why literacy, once smashed, must be left in the dust heap of history, its use never to be countenanced again.

The average reader, once they put this volume down, will not look at a book, magazine, or needlepoint motivational axiom again. Less pacific ones might take to the streets, demanding action and change. These protesters, unlike activists of the past, will *not* be holding or waving signs with painted slogans, though some traditionalists among them may still burn, loot, and smash things. A few commendable souls, not satiated by a single evening's outburst, might join the ranks of an analphabetic organization, one of the top-secret clubs that crusade for "de-education" and mass illiteracy. Regardless, some action of some sort will probably seem necessary.

The lazy ones will doubtlessly demur. "Well, I don't really read much anyway," they'll say. Or perhaps, with a harrumph, "No one really reads anymore." But that's a cop-out. Because after reading this book, the incandescent will understand that *not reading* is *not enough*. Instead we must go beyond illiteracy to "antiliteracy." Antiliteracy is a principled stance against literature, against the literate, against the phonetic alphabet, and against the printed word. Because, though never acknowledged and not completely understood, the power of the printed word is as awesome as it is dangerous, more destructive than any nuclear arsenal, more addictive than any opiate, more insidious than any plague. We must address it in no uncertain terms with the strongest stuff we can muster.

II. THE PROGRAM OF MASS LITERACY

The ruling class is intent that every child, even the most disadvantaged, is taught their "ABCs." This is the only education that is absolutely compulsory. Everything else—science, math, art, sports—is essentially elective; just brown-nosing for college admission.

Why is the ruling class so concerned with our ability to read? They're not concerned with our health care. They're not concerned that we have shelter, food, or work. Or that we're not preyed upon by corporate confidence men, loan sharks, and rip-off artists. They're not concerned with protecting people from environmental degradation, junk food, addiction to prescription drugs, or being bombed or bullied by the military in countries that get out of line or require a "regime change." They're not concerned in any way, shape, or form with the health or livelihood of the people—unless it affects their bottom line—so why are they so intent on our literacy? Why is literacy so important to them, so venerated, so sanctified?

Though there may be some official platitudes mumbled about how it's vital for training the workforce and for all to lead a full life, etc., it's actually presented as a moral issue. And the morality on the matter is clear. To be illiterate is a shameful thing. If one is an analphabetic, one is a beast . . . or beneath a beast. Though there are some who cannot read among us, they live in the shadows, like communists or sexual deviants in the 1950s. Almost no one will cop to being an illiterate; doing so would be akin to confessing to a weakness for witchery in seventeenth-century Salem. It would mean banishment from society.

The credo of compulsory readership is imbued with religious tones of moralism and piety because literacy as a social requirement isn't enough. Scofflaws would backslide if it were just a law or ordinance. Instead, it's been decreed a sin not to read; dirty and degenerate. The elites need us to read so that we can read their propaganda; after all, the printed word conveys a sense of absolute authority and they enjoy a monopoly on its dissemination.

III. ". . . AND THE WORD WAS GOD"

The written word is unmatched in transmitting dictums from on high and organizing public opinion. Whether on the page, screen, or billboard, writing seems to come from an exalted place; anonymous, omniscient, and unimpeachable. It is the "voice of God" and it supersedes all else around it. When a person reads a book or news article, the written word's command over their consciousness is total. When in the writer's thrall, one is detached from family, friends, and one's milieu. Reading super-sedes hearing, smell, sense of space, and other environmental stimuli. It isolates a person; puts them in an escapist trance, a state that transports them to another world. In this world, the author can propose whatever rules of logic, whatever reality, and make any abstraction seem urgent and all-important. It gives the author, who often remains anonymous and institutional (in cases of news articles and advertising for example), a direct channel into the consciousness of the reader, through which they may douse the brain with nonsense of seemingly incontrovertible authority.

The primary use of the written word has always been indoctrination. The written word was first introduced into general society with the invention of the Gutenberg press, a device which, for the first time ever, allowed for mass proliferation of literature. Among its earliest uses was dissemination of Martin Luther's Protestant tracts, which led to the Reformation, the Christian schism, the Thirty Years' War, the religious wars, and the development of capitalism. From this crucible arose a new bourgeois elite who utilized the written word for their

Enlightenment insurrection against royalism. Literature indeed would be the principal weapon in the arsenal of the revolutionists. *Common Sense* by Thomas Paine was the top-selling pamphlet in the colonies immediately prior to the American Revolution, indispensable to the success of the 1776 gang. So much seditious matter was printed in France in the run-up to the 1789 insurrection that a special "book police" was formed by the king's government to monitor "bad books." The American and French revolutions both owed their success to the new word-weapons of the usurping capitalist class, the Masonic bourgeoisie who had eclipsed the titled nobility in wealth and now strove jealously for total control, over not just the state, but consciousness itself.

IV. SUPPRESS, REPRESS, DEPRESS . . . FREE PRESS

The power of the written word when proliferated is no secret; "The pen is mightier than the sword" is a bourgeois boast. Napoleon famously claimed to fear the press more than "one thousand bayonets." William Randolph Hearst's news machine famously initiated the Spanish-American War. "You furnish the pictures and I'll furnish the war," he quipped, and soon the United States annexed Puerto Rico, Cuba, and the Philippines from the Spanish crown. More recently, the *New York Times* has provided the liberal elite conscionable rationale for supporting the invasion of Afghanistan, the plunder of Iraq, the "War on Terror," the assassination of Qaddafi, sponsorship of the war in Syria, etc. The CIA calls the press "the mighty Wurlitzer," which it plays accordingly whenever manufacturing consent. Writing is the tool to tailor truth to a publisher's desire and disseminate a particular perspective. That the publishing houses and the newspapers are under monopolistic control by oligarchs (Bezos, Murdoch, the Vanguard group, BlackRock, et al.) and that the day's chosen news items reflect their ideological needs is never mentioned by the witless blowhards who hail the bravery of the reporter and the "sacred role" of a free press in democracy. Ballyhooed endlessly by the press itself, the journalist's self-aggrandizement as truth-seeking crusader is as specious and inverted as it is corny and tedious.

Literacy was trumpeted by its wretched apostles as indispensable to a people's "self-determination." But, in fact, readers aren't determining but are *being determined*. Their ideology is cultivated and pruned by the propaganda they're inculcated with, whether book, blurb, bulletin, or "news"— that most execrable form of writing which, in the Digital Age, is more ubiquitous than ever. Written words arrange our thoughts, subvert our intuition, and make our choices. We are flies in their author's web and, once pumped with their poison, our discourse resembles the rote melody of a player piano; a dutiful recital of facts, figures, and opinions courtesy of words, which, once printed in "black and white," seem irrefutable. Their uniform size, mesmerizing repetition, and stylish arrangement drug the reader into believing whatever they infer, no matter how outlandish, senseless, or idiotic. "Two Minutes Hate" against the bogeyman of the hour? Okay. Drop a bomb on the enemy population of the week? Well, certainly, yes, of course, if the venerable newspaper's op-ed says it's the thing to do.

Once one has been forced to understand the phonetic alphabet, one is unable to ignore the barrage of propaganda from books, billboards, broadsides, and skywriting biplanes at the beach. Though we affect a casual disregard for this "media," and shrug it off as tabloid fluff, clickbait, and sensationalism, it's actually immensely powerful. Like yeast in flour, words fester, burrow, and grow in our brain, and before we know it, we are under the spell of the scribes. We cannot help but recite their righteous diatribes, ad copy, or the informed op-ed they poured into our head this morning, even though it might contradict last week's screed. In each instance, we are programmed to parrot ruling-class ideology as if it sprang from our own brow. Yes, literate man is a cosmic dupe. His opinions, formed by cherry-picked data and fed to him by media and advertising conglomerates, are non sequitur Dada absurdities, aphasic art justice newspeak cum emotional therapy patriot drivel, or whatever the ruling class requires of him or her this week. This is what the modern literate is trained for. His entire education was designed to make him a herald for the elite's follies and frolics. Bred like a racehorse to promulgate their will and carry out their program. He has been subject to the mesmeric effects of print and type since before he can even remember.

V. LITERACY: MANKIND'S HANDICAP

Literate man is, indeed, the victim of every sort of manipulation. He or she, due to their learning, is almost defenseless. Mankind, after all, is born with certain natural defenses; one of them is *ignorance*. When Enlightenment ideology spread the gospel of "universal literacy," man, once benighted and strong, became literate and weak. Once one learns how to read and becomes a reader, one is stripped of sense; helpless to resist the whims of the word-smiths. In fact, the more literate one is, the more susceptible to suggestion, the more malleable one's mind. While the half-literate dum-dum still possibly harbors a healthy suspicion of the ruling class's latest prestidigitation, in the arena of academia the PhD student can be made to believe anything.

The word's dominance over us, its master role in our relationship, is nothing to be surprised by. The written word seems to be truth itself; particularly if the right typeface is used and the words are arranged just so. And one can't escape words. They jump out and inflict themselves on us like flashers in the night. On billboards, in books, and the buzzing alerts from the telecommunications hardware that occupies each of our pockets.

Even this piece of writing, the one you are presently reading, is attempting to rally you, persuade you, affect your thoughts and actions. But—this one, this piece of writing you're reading now, is different than all the rest. It constitutes the most important piece of text you will ever read; above Shakespeare, Milton, and Joyce. Indeed, you are quite fortunate to be privy to its special blend of truth and taboo. Because these words aren't designed to *perpetuate* the reading of words but instead to *end* the reading of words. To inspire the reader henceforth to never read another piece of writing ever again.

VI. THE CAMP FOR DE-EDUCATION

With this final piece of writing, the written word's reign is finally over.

These words are designed to convince the reader to stop reading anything ever again. And not only to stop reading, but to forget how to read. Reading is not like a bicycle. We can unlearn it. The Chinese Communists, during the "Cultural Revolution," had camps for "reeducation," to unlearn the counterrevolutionary programming of the former regime. But this is not that. This is an exhortation—not for "reeducation"—but for *de-education*. Unlearning, and then not learning anything to replace what you have unlearned. Written words, after all, are vile servants of the ruling class whose only objective is to enslave you. To pry them from our consciousness, to unlearn letters, spelling, punctuation, and sentence structure, not to mention all the foul lessons we've learned through them, the vile sophistry and nonsense, will be a tough task certainly. But not too tough for those committed to antiliteracy and de-education.

Some well-meaning souls will doubtlessly protest, saying, "Don't throw the baby out with the bathwater," and other such alliterative saws. And sure, words could be used—and once were—for poetry and love. But now they are firmly in the service of degenerate "news" media and advertising, twin demons which are almost interchangeable. Therefore, there can be no compromise. We must be sure to keep written words from our children, so that they are illiterate from the start and never fall sway to the sicko agenda of the dissolute oligarchs who have harnessed the alphabet to serve at their pleasure.

Why did we learn to read? We had no choice. It was compulsory. Forced upon us when we were just babes, absolutely impressionable, without the agency, wisdom, or foresight to understand just what it would mean to be a "reader": another goon, another dupe, another goose-stepping soldier in the army of letters. We didn't understand that it would mean a lifetime spent in the prison of literacy, and that the con men in advertising and news media now had a direct mineshaft into our previously cloistered cavern of consciousness. We were now a jukebox that would play whatever tune they wanted. People of the future may judge us, call us stupid and naive, but we didn't know any better. We were children and hadn't the life experience to make an educated decision not to learn how to read. The ramifications of literacy weren't even discussed. And now it's too late; we're caught in a penitentiary of lies and deceit.

To think: we were so proud to learn. When we were little, we boasted about the "reading level" we had attained, and gloated over having finished epics such as *The Lord of the Rings* or *Watership Down*. We were taught that reading a book, regardless of how negligible or stupid, comprised a noble act; how it was proof of moral rectitude, intelligence, and class. It made us superior. But where did this education actually get us? We find that we don't spend our time with Chaucer, Zora Neale Hurston, or Borges, but are instead hypnotized by the barrage of mind control and brain contamination the oligarchs commission as our daily intake.

The young child is immediately taught a hierarchical system called "the alphabet." The letters themselves represent a hierarchy of sounds, which is a matter for reformation in and of itself. Its arbitrarily ranked arrangements—*A, B, C . . .*—with only a paucity of "vowels," stymies expression, and many sounds, which should by all rights be words, are nowhere to be found in a dictionary. Why are words and expressions only sounds made with the tongue? Why not the ruminations of the stomach for example?

Once they are indoctrinated with letters, then the words are introduced. Reading is soon to follow. Reading takes them away from experience and forces them to live in the abstract. They no longer experience the world but a projection by an author or writer. They start to live a fantasy, which is sold as sophisticated. To take on the perspective of the writer, who is supposed to be an authentic source of information. The library is a kind of opium den; the bookstore, a combination of boot camp and brothel. But instead of prostitutes who provide sensual attention to the lonely, ugly, and undeserving, the consorts are tomes; seedy promulgators of ideology, of escapism, of mind-corrupting philosophy.

VII. THE TERRIBLE ORIGINS OF THE WRITTEN WORD

The first written languages were runes, glyphs, and sacred texts that were only known to a few. These written languages were more innocuous than their contemporary counterparts since they weren't commonly understood and were broken out only for rituals and special occasions.

The book was an impressive prop in the hands of a holy man, but since it was only decipherable by a sanctified class of priests, specially equipped to handle its terrifying potency, it was essentially mumbo jumbo; a totem to signify importance, not unlike scientific or academic art jargon nowadays. Writing was regarded with a reverence befitting its extraordinary power. Letters were used of course—for holy languages—but not for the "lay" dialects which people actually spoke.

When the Gutenberg press—the earliest printing press—was invented, books were suddenly disseminated in mass quantities, produced for the first time in people's spoken tongues, not just Latin, Quranic Arabic, or Chinese ideograms. In a language group then, whatever dialect was typically used for literature became the "standard"(e.g., Florentine Italian) and other tongues became lesser, in a hierarchy of correctness, which typically reflected economic conditions. This phenomenon served to corral the speakers of disparate dialects into larger language-based identities, a trend which eventually resulted in "nationalism." Under nationalism, dialects were suppressed and even outlawed when one version of a language was institutionalized as paradigmatic over all others.

The press was initially used to spread the ideas of the Reformation through Europe. Capitalism, the dog-eat-dog religion of selfishness and exploitation—a mutation of Protestantism—is another wretched offspring of Gutenberg and, more specifically, the printed word. The Industrial Revolution, the capitalist's project to transform the world into a machine to extract profit from any possible source, was also a direct result of Gutenberg's invention. The Gutenberg press was responsible, therefore, not just for "media," but also for Protestantism, nationalism, the nation-state, cultural hegemony, modern imperialism, and the Industrial Revolution.

Universal literacy—turning man's mind into a machine—was not far behind.

Literacy was hawked as a way for workers to help liberate themselves and determine their own fate. But, in fact, mass literacy was a project to involve the proletariat in their own enslavement. Instead of having a distinct culture from the aristocracy, as had been the case in the past, they became the fan club, wannabes, and flunky facilitators of the new moneyed "middle" class who, through novels, newspapers, and tabloids, demarcated and explained the new ideology and its stringent set of morality and ethics. The "Protestant ethic" was a new religion, the tenets of which were that wealth was proof of virtue while poverty revealed the poor's intrinsic moral pollution. The exaltation of mass literacy was tied into Enlightenment thinking; science as a new divinity. While under the Church everyone had a place in God's master plan and the poor were ennobled, under bourgeois ideology one only had oneself to blame for one's misfortune. Psychically, the American malaise can be chalked up to the collective shame of the working class for not being filthy rich.

VIII. ANTIDOTE TO LANGUAGE

The hurdle confronting those antiliterates who are dedicated to a program of de-education is that the temptation to spell is overwhelming. Therefore, the antidote might be to first find a language that has no actual words and cannot be spelled, thereby liberating humanity from the specter of the written word, which—while language exists—can be reconstituted by sinister forces at any juncture and used to repress and control society as before.

Though this sounds outrageous, this language is already here. The template is already with us in the form of a language which resembles the Latin of the Middle Ages or the Arabic of Islam; a universal tongue of magical nonsense that cannot be spelled out or standardized or balkanized like the local dialects which were suppressed or institutionalized by the nationalist movements. This language is *rock 'n' roll*.

Rock 'n' roll was a universal language that required no literacy. One that united its followers under an ideological umbrella, regardless of language, creed, or culture. Its membership was understood and inferred. It represented a vague aesthetic and an even more vague set of values. But when one rock 'n' roller saw another, there was an understanding, despite whatever lack of common language or background. Their respective cultures may have been remote, but their collective tongue of beats, shouts, and devil-may-care cacophony would provide a sense of recognition, kinship, and understanding. A rock 'n' roller from Japan was therefore linked more profoundly to a rock 'n' roller from Ohio, Lagos, or Lima, for example, than they were to coeds, colleagues, or even family.

Rock 'n' roll had no written language. When it began, in particular, it consisted of gobbledygook: *wop bop a loo bop, rama lama ding dong, bebop a lula,* etc.; made-up sounds which were a replacement for language; a refutation of "The Word" and its meaning, of coherence, and the constraints and controls of language itself. It was a replacement for bourgeois discourse and represented a new type of language, without words.

When rock 'n' roll defied language, it became a competing religion. "The Word," after all, is God. In the Bible, John 1:1 specifically states: *First there was the Word and the Word was God.* When rock 'n' roll put down the word, asserted that "the bird is the word," and other non-sequitur inanities, it rendered language obsolete and, in so doing, took God's place. It became a new god. A new god or perhaps the long-awaited reincarnation of an ancient, primordial ur-deity, the amoral entity that had preceded the respectable and didactic law-giving God of the various holy books' respective faiths; perhaps akin to the titans that lived before Zeus.

Rock 'n' roll not only made language obsolete but also time. After all, *First there was the Word and the Word was God.* Language, the word, was "first"; the *initial event* of time. Therefore, that which obliterates language also obliterates time. So when rock 'n' roll was dug up from the ancient unconscious, resurrected and then reintroduced as a language above and beyond words, it was also something timeless, living before, after, outside of time; in the eternal cosmos.

Rock 'n' roll replaced "The Word." In the beginning there had been "The Word." "The Word" was necessary for things to exist; language is the integral component for creation. "The Word" preceded all else in the Bible. "The Word" had been "God"; God was a *WORD*. Regardless of the religion, language is the deity.

Rock 'n' roll is the refutation of language. *Bop bop a shoo bop* and Little Richard's nonsense language is a refutation therefore of God. Rock 'n' roll is salvation from the poison of the printed word.

Not only is rock 'n' roll the antidote to the written word, but rock 'n' roll can also help us *not* to read. The distraction and cacophony it provides make it almost impossible to concentrate on whatever bilious propaganda one is being force-fed, whether it be text message, news feed, or magazine article. It confuses, distracts, makes the job of reading a chore instead of a compulsion. So turn it up! We need more of this dissonant nonsense.

Of course, rock 'n' roll—this mystical, cosmic force—while a great tool for antiliterates in the coming war against reading, has its own checkered past.

Like oil, water, and Ouija boards, rock 'n' roll was, during the "postwar" period of the twentieth century, exploited, perverted, and packaged by capitalists. As such, it was enormously influential and even utilized overseas as a propaganda weapon, to be used as an envoy of neoliberal "Western" ideology during the Cold War. The ancient and indefinable was alchemized into plastic, publishing, and agitprop. As such, it was required to take a "flesh" form, and sit amongst the other salable and quantifiable elements of the market.

Thus, that which was totally timeless, ancient, futuristic, and immovable became not just polluted with time, but synonymous with time. Records were 33 rpm or 45 rpm and rock 'n' roll fans rocked "around the clock." Because rock 'n' roll was adopted as the mascot and mouthpiece of the "boomer" age group, the music's demeanor in every era was supposed to correspond to the concurrent life stage of that particular postwar generation. For example, rock 'n' roll from the '50s is popularly thought to be for young kids and teens. In the '60s, rock 'n' roll was for college types, and twentysomethings, while in the '70s "rock" became a been-there-done-that soundtrack for jaded divorcées and young professionals. In the 1980s, the music was middle-aged, knowing, corporate, and suburban; concerned with nostalgic reenactments of adolescent glory (Bob Seger's "Night Moves," Don Henley's "The Boys of Summer," Bryan Adams's "Summer of '69," Eddie Money's "Take Me Home Tonight," Jefferson Starship's "We Built This City"). The punk era (1976–78), therefore, represents a midlife crisis and was alternately celebrated and reviled by the form's old guard ("Rough Boys" by Pete Townshend, "Shattered" by the Rolling Stones, "Predictable" by the Kinks, "It's Still Rock and Roll to Me" by Billy Joel), who took turns denouncing it and laying claim to it.

Rock 'n' roll got caught up in the myth of history as well, and its political significance with regard to the Cold War, America's postwar imperial primacy, postindustrial consumer society, pharmaceutical developments in birth control, and the neoliberal's fair-weather relationship with religion and nationalism.

Now, though, the "baby boom" generation has burned out and the music has mirrored this collapse. They've let go the leash on the music they harnessed for so long. Rock 'n' roll is meanwhile irrelevant to a culture industry which has moved on to other, more efficient mind-control modes, and which no longer has any use for it.

As an obsolete, near-forgotten technology, then, rock 'n' roll can finally be utilized for its intended purpose, the one for which it was originally feared and loathed: its power to create illiteracy in its followers. Having lain in the ground for years as a dormant corpse, it can now rise again, free of the bad associations the music industry and intelligence agencies saddled it with, ready for rehabilitation, redemption, and retribution.

Through the applied use of rock 'n' roll, we can move not only away from the written word, but also from language itself, and free ourselves from its deadly grip.

FIN

The Grand Tour

2

THE GRAND TOUR

The Neoliberal Army
Pays Its Own Way

At first glance, "tourism" is an economic model; a commercial enterprise based on taking a population *away from their things*—their home, their car, their kitchen, and their community—and placing them as "tourists" in a foreign environment, where they must forage for food, lodging, transport, and things to do, to occupy their time.

On any summer day in Venice, for example, there are up to 80,000 of these lost souls stumbling around the Grand Canal: cold, hungry, and indigent, searching for a purpose, a pastime, a reason to be. Their plight is mirrored across Italy.

An average of 257,300 tourists shuffle through

the country's cathedrals, palazzi, and ancient ruins daily, with Rome and Florence being the most hard hit. Paris also endures hordes of *visiteurs étrangers,* and must barrack and feed around 100,000 of them every night in the summer months. All of them are looking for "R & R" in the form of crumbling castles, old churches, grand vistas, and the cozy-exotic.

Wherever they go, tourists are distinct from the local population. They live in a parallel dimension, which coexists but rarely collides with the life of normal civilians. In this dimension, they are treated with special regard. The world's most desirable beaches and old-city districts are for their exclusive use, along with the Vatican, Pyramids, Acropolis, Taj Mahal, et al.

These invaders, who come to command the economies and define the cultures of the places they visit, dwarf historic armies of renown in their size and strength. Rommel, the "Desert Fox," for example, battled the Allies in Cyrenaica with fewer than 80,000 "Afrika Korps." Napoleon's Grande Armée of chasseurs, grenadiers, and cuirassiers at Waterloo counted 72,000. And Hannibal led only

26,000 Carthaginians on his famous Alpine elephant excursion to humble Rome.

William conquered Harold at Hastings with 7,000 Normans, the CIA-backed revanchists at the "Bay of Pigs" mustered a mere 1,400 *"gusanos,"* and Fidel Castro won Cuba two years earlier with a guerrilla force of just 200 *"barbudos."* All of these armies seem quaint when contrasted with the backpacked hordes that storm the Eiffel Tower each afternoon in June.

Tourists, like soldiers, are shorn of individual identity. Their dress, destinations, and demeanor all resemble one another's, with tourism transforming them into a kind of fanny-packed phalanx, with a militaristic hive mind. The touristic propaganda they consume en route to their vacation destination is a kind of indoctrination; a soft boot camp that tailors their expectations, attitudes, and goals for the places they will occupy.

In the army, the buzz cut, olive drab outfits, drills, marches, and ideological "basic training" are designed not for acumen on the battlefield as much as to erase the soldier's ego and ingratiate them into the organization which acts as "enforcer" of the nation's economic agenda.

Thus, when the soldier is "deployed," they are no longer so-and-so from Idaho who drives a Camaro, but an indoctrinated GI Joe who does what they're told. The platoon, or "band of brothers," is the soldier's family overseas. This family has its own myths, values, and patriarch, as well as its own family business: enforcing its nation's imperial will, either through violence or the threat of violence.

Sometimes actual conflict occurs ("war"), but typically the invocation of violence is sufficient for extortion, provided the extortionist government has a track record of barbarity and can stake a plausible claim to sadism and cynical realpolitik (e.g., Hiroshima).

Regardless, when the soldier is discharged, they will have gained worldliness, having been stationed overseas. This promise of sophistication has been the allure of the military for centuries. The Swedish Viking youths in the tenth century who went to serve the Byzantine emperor as the Varangian Guard were mythic in their native land, the subject of many a rune-stone. *Join the Navy and see the World* was the recruitment pitch of the last century, and American veterans of the war in Vietnam typically commissioned a satin jacket emblazoned with the circumstances of their time overseas: unit number, years of service, places stationed, et al., topped off with some wry sentiment of antiauthoritarian fatalism.

At sports events, airports, and ice cream parlors, the veteran or serviceperson is genuflected before, and regarded with official displays of near holy reverence. Whether they saw combat or not, they put themselves in danger for us, or so the saw goes. Regardless of what your politics are, or what they were actually doing, the soldier is supposed to be the outer defensive crust of the collective "us." Whatever they are doing now, when they were in uniform, they were our exoskeleton; they put themselves in harm's way instead of us, and for our sake. As with Christ on the cross "dying for our sins" or other various patriotic homilies, the logic is unclear as to exactly what we are thankful for, but every civilian does feel genuine relief that the soldier went through this crucible—the metamorphosis of the individual into unquestioning exponent and potential sacrifice of the state—instead of them.

Like the soldier, the tourist is also transformed,

through the act of tourism, from an individual into an exponent of their nation and/or class, and enforcer of its ideology.

But while the soldier is working class, the tourist is bourgeois. At home, the tourist, raised on the capitalist ideology of "heroic individualism," espouses various likes, dislikes, and "personal beliefs." These are carefully honed to display a blend of reason and sensible conformity on the one hand (important for likability, employment, and mating), with a pinch of perversity and impertinence on the other (to show that they are free-thinking and nobody's fool; also vital components for successful coupling). With this constructed identity and "personality," they define and contrast themselves against neighbors, family, friends, and society at large. In a foreign land, however, these affectations lose value, and become meaningless. The tourist feels lost and unremarkable, and deigns to hang around countrymen they would normally eschew with snobbish contempt. Marching through the old town of the foreign city with their tourist cohort, the once proud individual is as distinct as a bee in a swarm.

The reduction of the tourist into an emblem of their particular class and place of origin is quite dramatic, as is their willingness to leave their possessions, which constitute some of their primary sources of identity and power. The tourist in their natural habitat is housed, clothed, and capable of cooking in their own kitchen. They also typically transport themselves in their own automobiles. As a tourist, though, out of dutiful adherence to the bourgeois edict of attaining "worldliness," they render themselves homeless, car-less, hungry, and helpless. They hurl themselves into an exotic environ where they are disoriented, dumb, and confused. Their days abroad are existential; empty voids they seek to fill, either with consumerist debauchery or "culture."

Historically, the reasons for military conquest would be to gain a nation's wealth, treasure, sophistication (e.g., the culture of Byzantium, coveted by the Crusaders and Turks), resources (as with the German attempt to conquer Russia or the USA's invasion of Iraq), or its strategic position on the map (such as Malta for the British or Afghanistan for NATO). With tourism it's the same. The tourist is on an expedition, either to consume cultural wealth (such as art, architecture, etc.), natural splendor (a beach or mountain range), or visit a place that strategically positions them in a particular social context (e.g., Tulum, St. Tropez, Marrakech in the 1960s). The food and drink of a place, also a concern for the tourist, could be considered both cultural wealth and resource. Tourist agencies often invent new cultural treasures and attractions and use these to dispatch tourists to ever more remote outposts such as Iceland, which was, until recently, thought of as a barren volcanic rock shrouded in darkness, whose inhabitants ate fermented shark, but is now a trendy top-shelf destination.

When vacation is over and the tourist is discharged from their tour of duty, they return home with anecdotes, insights, and a bag laden with souvenirs. They are already planning their next expedition. Meanwhile, another tourist, indistinguishable from them, dutifully patrols the landmarks, cultural treasures, and/or natural splendor of whatever vacation spot they just left. Though they seem compelled to "tour" for romance, wanderlust, and to gain social credit, there is another impulse at work. The tourist is compelled to tour because doing so serves a strategic role for the system, economy, and state, of which they are an exponent.

The tourist serves as part of a colonizing army. In previous eras, one nation might invade and occupy another, and thus gain proprietary economic advantages over their fallen foe. Sometimes there would be an enduring military presence in the beaten land to enforce submission—an "occupation."

The Romans had fortresses across North Africa, the Near East, and Europe. Moorish castles still stand in Grenada, and English castles dot the Celtic landscape in Wales. The USA has fortresses too: Fort Wayne, Fort Worth, and Fort Lauderdale are among many army bases built to conquer, suppress, and expel indigenous people during the United States' insatiable expansion; the so-called "Winning of the West."

US army bases have been a feature around the globe, from Okinawa to Italy, ever since WWII, established under the postwar pretext of "containing communism." The "War on Terror" and invasion of Afghanistan created the opportunity to erect more military installations, in theretofore-inaccessible ex-Soviet nations like Uzbekistan. But army bases are ungainly, unpopular, and can only do so much. The USA's 750+ overseas military bases are expensive to maintain as well, and the personnel—culled from the poorest and least reconstructed sectors of society—are sometimes a liability, as they can be drunk and disorderly, go AWOL, or what have you. Therefore, while army bases are effective for ensuring the submission of a beaten foe, a different sort of "boots on the ground" is required for more comprehensive occupation.

The tourist is perfect for this role: guileless and idealistic, curious about the place they visit, and representing the most respectable class of their mother country. They serve to spread the values of their homeland and, through their patronage, cultivate these aesthetics and concepts wherever they go. The hotels they use, the restaurants that serve them, and the cabs they hail must meet the platonic ideals they enforce through their patronage.

The tourists are a multinational occupying force, and represent a pan-bourgeois army, spreading middle-class values, morality, customs, aesthetics, and material standards wherever they go. Just as Hitler's Wehrmacht was a polyglot, comprising soldiers from across the Reich—the Charlemagne SS Division from France, the Viking and Nordland SS divisions from Scandinavia, the Ukrainian "Nightingale" battalion, and the Blue Legion from Spain, among others—who united under the banner of fascism, Russophobia, anti-Semitism, and anticommunism; and just as Napoleon incorporated men-at-arms from across his empire to spread the Enlightenment ideals of the "Code Napoleon," the tourist is also part of a "Grande Armée" who hail from different nations, but share a bourgeois sensibility and value system.

The tourist is as effective in spreading neoliberal values as Mohammed's horsemen were in spreading Islam across the Middle East and North Africa during their whirlwind conquests. The tourist, though ostensibly spurning their homeland and imbued with a curiosity for the foreign and exotic, actually brings their culture, their morality, their digital technology, and their aesthetics with them, and, with the totalitarianism intrinsic to the market, enforces their institution "on the ground."

The tourist is therefore an indispensable stra-

tegic asset, not only as a diplomat and an occupying centurion, but one who—in the neoliberal
tradition—pays for their own bed and board. Yes,
the tourist is a member of an occupying force that
maintains a foothold on foreign soil, but at great
cost to themselves. Like the "adjuncts" and grad-
uate students who replaced tenured professors
during the neoliberal university putsch, or the mil-
lennial interns whose free labor enabled the purge
of salaried writers, designers, and photographers at
media conglomerates during the digital coup, or
Silicon Valley's transformed workforce of dispos-
able beggars ("gig workers") who have no security,
pension, or health care (e.g., Uber and Instacart
drivers), the tourist is the neoliberal's GI Joe, who
bivouacs for the tech-capitalist fatherland, but on
their own dime. These DIY troopers don't enjoy
the meager perks of the military, such as C rations,
C-130 transport planes, base camps, or any kind
of esprit de corps. Instead they must organize and
foot the bill for every aspect of their own D-Day
invasion.

The tourist is responsible for themself, and is
never rewarded for their time in the field with the

medals, citations, pensions, or benefits of the normal serviceman or -woman. Despite the fact that their work is many times more vital to the project of imperialism than the old-fashioned dogface sitting on their ass back at base. After all, the soldier—though they might hit the town on "R & R" and raise some hell—is a pariah, stuck in a uniform, unable to effectively infiltrate or influence. These khaki-wearing dinosaurs are quaint relics of an old type of imperialism, which has been almost entirely replaced by the new-model army of culture-vulture jet-set boutique-hotel tourist commandos, whose nouveau Omaha Beach is equipped with a tequila bar and whose Pork Chop Hill is a Michelin restaurant. Already, Germany is dotted with abandoned army barracks, and the brothels that once served them are cold and shuttered. Soon we shall see the last of these old-timey garrisons fade out of sight, replaced by Airbnb's and luxury resorts that will house the tourist occupation army that does the work of its olive-drab predecessor in a manner which better suits the miserly libertarian austerity despots who run the G7, IMF, and World Bank.

The occupation paradigm used to be one of

requisitioning the best property and using it for the high command and barracks of the invaders. During the Nazi occupation of Paris, for example, the Luftwaffe took the Ritz, the German navy moved into the Hôtel de la Marine, German intelligence annexed the Hôtel Lutetia, and the German high command took the Majestic Hotel as their headquarters. Particular bordellos, cabarets, cinemas, and cafés became the playground for an exclusively German clientele, as every Wehrmacht soldier was promised a minimum of one leave in Paris.

After Germany lost the war, the USA established its occupation headquarters in picturesque Heidelberg, a city with a delightful medieval bridge, a Rosicrucian Renaissance garden (Hortus Palatinus), and historical significance as the center of the German Romantic movement. With an eye to an extended stay there in the future, the Americans had spared it the carpet-bombing that had laid waste to the rest of the country. Similarly, during the French conquest of Egypt, Napoleon's science-and-arts entourage annexed the elegant Ottoman Palace, Bayt al-Sinnari, and in Iraq the US's military brass, mercenary contractors, and oilmen bunked at Saddam's modernist Republican Palace in the tony colonizers-only Baghdad neighborhood they called the "Green Zone."

The modern tourist, as the premiere agent for the ongoing imperial conquest by stateless neoliberal global capitalists, also takes the best property in every city they invade. With the new "Airbnb" paradigm, this means the most sought-after neighborhoods are off-limits to locals; the exclusive domain of an Instagramming jet-set elite. The industries they patronize also annex the most valued properties; the Paris Opera House is entirely occupied by a cavernous Apple store, for example.

While we can see that tourists are a kind of covert soldiery, soldiers are tourists too.

One could view Napoleon, Alexander the Great, Richard Lionheart, and Douglas MacArthur this way. The Vikings, Huns, and Mongol horde were all sightseers and curiosity seekers, who pillaged and conquered in a manner not dissimilar to beachgoers in Cancún or Bora-Bora. The Corinthians who invaded Syracuse were like the modern moneyed expats who just need a getaway. Julius

Caesar's war journals, the *Commentāriī de Bello Gallicō,* read as travelogs, in which he regales the reader with accounts of the Druids, Gauls, Aquitani, and Germans he encountered on his campaigns.

The Crusades were composed of pilgrims, eager to ogle the holy places. When Napoleon went to Egypt, he brought hundreds of scholars and scientists; Masonic Egyptologists intent on cataloging the treasures of the pharaohs, not unlike the sightseers who crowd the British Museum to gawk at those same items nowadays. Reichsmarschall Göring was a collector whose "blitzkrieg" of Europe was, for him, principally a method of collecting rare paintings and sculpture. Many modern tourists are collectors as well, and their travels facilitate similar shopping yens. The US annexation of Hawaii was motivated by a desire to control the Pacific militarily and economically, but it also ensured the best waves for surfing were in US territory, extending Monroe's "locals only" doctrine to include Surf City. And the Spanish Civil War was the ultimate touristic event, with oodles of adventure seekers from all over Europe going to bear arms under the Catalonian sun, while Hemingway and

Orwell scribbled travel reports from the front lines. Like that war, which was chic for leftists, tourism is always tinged with a political/aesthetic aspect with regard to what it means, where one goes.

Though this seems like a radical shift of the military-occupation paradigm, we see the tourist and the soldier aren't that different. In fact, the two are twins in a bipartite attack. After the soldier storms the beach, the tourist maintains its pacification, through clueless passive-aggressive occupation. While the soldier uses arms, the tourist's cudgel is their dollar, and the monetary incentive they give the colonized to continue their servitude. While the soldier seizes the wealth of a country, the tourist pumps up the value of that treasure. The bounty of a nation and its "culture," after all, are the things that give the place its worth. If a place is cleaned of loot, it's no longer an asset for its conqueror. If the treasure is codified, mythologized, and nationalized, though—as with the Colosseum, the Pyramids, or the treasures of the Louvre—the place retains value and profits are guaranteed to increase. Invasion is not unlike the modern real estate market in this respect.

When Western Europe was conquered by the USA in 1945, theretofore undesirable places such as Iceland, Belgium, and the Netherlands became touristic destinations for Americans who continued a de facto occupation that exists to the present day. Eastern Europe, which had been annexed by the Soviet Union, was déclassé to these same pleasure seekers, despite the fact that the Black Sea, Budapest, Prague, and Kyiv were at least as culturally rich as touristic hot spots like Munich, Brussels, and Dublin. Once the Soviet Union was sold out and defeated by a combination of Cold War attrition and internal treachery, the East was overrun with tourists, who occupied the perimeter in a manner the anticommunist crusaders of NATO had always dreamed of doing, but never could.

Because the value of a country is rated by the strength of its tourist trade, many nations contrive cultural wealth and resources to attract tourist invasion and occupation. The "culture" a country can concoct for itself is the lure for this tourism. When a country hasn't got a Colosseum or an Eiffel Tower, it must invent some other attraction for the occupier. Can the country make a compelling case for itself as a cultural place? What does culture consist of? At this point, provided it has the right sales pitch, it can be almost anything; an inhospitable environment or a price tag that makes it exclusive (as seen with the recent craze for space tourism).

As with the old prohibition against traveling to the USSR, tourism is still officially discouraged in enemy countries that haven't been subdued entirely to the global capitalist hegemon, such as Iran, Cuba, and North Korea, places which are flagged with fearful travel advisories.

With the advent of the Internet—the ultimate colonizer—the tourist's job has become more efficient but also less vital. The Internet dictates standardization and conformity and can work hand in hand with the tourist, maximizing their economic influence, but it also threatens the tourist's role as soft centurion.

The Internet is the same almost everywhere you go, and it enforces sameness in the world it occupies. With this "Imperialist-ernet," once-exotic destinations have become indistinct from one another in an arms race of conformity to a global standard of luxury-brand diversity street-wear, and corporate-sponsored celebrity skateboarding. There is less and less incentive to travel, because everywhere is an indistinguishable worldwide webscape, accessible from anywhere, which can be homogenized and policed remotely. More and more, the tourist's mission overseas seems redundant and unnecessary.

The tourist—who has never been officially recognized for their selfless service to the state—faces an inevitable phasing out, like their GI predecessor suffers now, if restrictions on global net-surfing aren't put into place. Just as the flower of French knighthood was extinguished at the hands of vulgar archers at the battles of Crecy and Agincourt, the tourist will be replaced by decidedly nonadventurous virtual technology. And the tourist, having insisted on the latest Wi-Fi and computer technology at their remote Himalayan getaway and blissful island paradise, has played the key role in implementing their own obsolescence.

So, though the sightseer still stubbornly sallies forth into battle, with the doughty spirit for which he or she is renowned, they do so wistfully, knowing their days are numbered. The writing is on the wall; the brave tourist-soldier may soon be like the knights of yore: a legend and nothing more.

FIN

How
I
Survived
Re-
Education
Camp

3

"I SURVIVED REEDUCATION CAMP"

A Workshop on Brainwashing, Mind Control, and Songwriting

[Note: This lecture is transcribed from a reeducation workshop held by the author at a Southern California music festival.]

FESTIVAL REPRESENTATIVE: Hello, festival-goers. Welcome to the talk. Today's reeducation camp workshop focuses on the craft of songwriting. Please welcome the famous lecturer.

AUDIENCE: [Vigorous applause.]

LECTURER: Hello and welcome to the camp. The

brainwashing camp for reeducation. Is everyone comfortable? Did everyone get a shirt? Later, I'm going to need you to take these little pills. They are placebos technically, but studies have shown that ingesting them will help make you more compliant and susceptible to the messages we are sharing.

Today we're going to teach you—normally the hapless target of mind controllers—how to get into the game of mind controlling others. We're also going to reeducate you and give you ideological training, much needed after all the brainwashing you've been subjected to.

As you know, the reason you're here at the festival is because you were compelled to be here. What compelled you? Music. You were brought here by music. You had no choice. The most potent tool for mind control is repetition or "music." That's right: music is the number one most effective tool for mind control.

Why do religions use psalms? Why do cults have mantras? Why do nation-states use anthems and advertising agencies license songs? Because you can never shake a jingle once you've learned it. Once it's crept into your consciousness, you're a disciple.

Its message infiltrates your unconscious, burrows into your psyche, and is almost impossible to expel. All successful cults have a musical element; from the Source Family to the Manson Family, from the Branch Davidians to the Catholic Church, and so on. We too shall use music.

Music

Rock 'n' roll has always been a reeducation camp; a revolutionary tool. Its ability to capture imagination, steer thought, and control behavior is well documented and nearly unparalleled. Of course, it's often misused, corrupted, utilized by nefarious forces. But that doesn't mean it's intrinsically bad, just that it's versatile.

Amplified music, either recorded or played live, will be the reeducation camp we use to rehabilitate the enemy population, a way for them to atone for their hideous crimes, too numerous to mention. Music is a weapon, typically used against us, but one we can also use on our foes (who comprise most of humanity), provided we learn to master it.

Physical Exhaustion

One aspect of mind control, if you've ever been inducted into a cult, is physical exhaustion. When the body is exhausted, the mind cannot resist. So typically cults induce physical exhaustion, maybe through enforced standing for hours—such as at a rock show—or through sports or menial labor. This makes their followers passive and compliant.

When rock 'n' roll was becoming paradigmatic, dancing was enforced, as this exhausted the listener and made them more susceptible to the message of the music. Why do modern rock concerts feature interminable standing around with no available seating? Mind control.

Because of this, as part of our brainwashing workshop, we'll ask you to do some physical exertion at some point to make you more susceptible to suggestion and more willing to accept the lessons we are giving. Meanwhile, when creating your own mind control, rhythmic music works best. The more "danceable," the more effective. Resist the myth of mind/body duality, which is anathema to the rock 'n' roll creed. Remember: an exhausted body is an exhausted mind!

SONGWRITING TECHNIQUE

Step 1: Pills

First off, we have to ask you to take the pill. It's a placebo, absolutely harmless—the dreaded pharmaceutical industry had nothing to do with creating this pill and it won't make you high or anything, but if we take it together, it's a symbolic gateway to our new psychic reality and will help us all to wash our brains and get on message. It will also help forge a sense of communal trust or bonding, as we will have all gone through this fearful trauma together. It can help us forge an identity in opposition to all who didn't go through this experience.

Step 2: Message

Now that we are bonded as a community, we can express ourselves freely. What is the message we want to put forth? How do we want to brainwash people?

In advertising, the message is simple: *Buy this and you'll be more sexually potent*. In politics, the message is complacency, equivocation, etc. But we're going to go for a more nuanced approach with our brainwashing. We need it to be useful in another way; a subtle yet transformative message that spreads our program and undermines enemy ideology, a message to make the world more tolerable for us.

We're going to study some of the techniques that have been used on us via music, writing, and art.

Art is, at its root, a complaint. A complaint or proposal about reality which it attempts to anti-dote aesthetically or through suggestion. You need to determine what your complaint is. After this, you can spread your complaint to the world.

On the paper provided, I'd like you to write down three things:

First, a complaint you have . . . This could be a complaint with the culture, your situation, your friends, even with this lecture.

Second, you can write a way this makes you feel, in one or two words.

Third, you can write down a solution to this problem. It can be improbable or practical. It can be pure fantasy. Keep it brief.

1. PROBLEM: This will be the "verse."
2. FEELING: This will be the "pre-chorus."
3. SOLUTION: This will be the "chorus."

While the pop song formula varies occasionally, for our purposes *three* is the number. You will use three verses, three choruses, three chords, and a coda will repeat thrice as the song fades out and the message is hammered home.

If you did it correctly, each one of you will have now composed an archetypal pop song. When read aloud, your song will be revealed. Though one's impulse might be to embellish this austere composition so as to display one's wit and mastery of language, it's best to keep it simple. Repetition—incessant and interminable—will be the key to your tune's success; not poetry.

You now have the basic structure of your initial pop complaint. With a little arrangement, some luck, and a bit of fine-tuning, it could be a hit.

Step 3. Repetition of Message
As I mentioned, repetition is the absolutely vital

component for mind control to be effective. When one thinks of one's own indoctrination, whether it's via capitalist consumer culture, the patriarchy, social media, the Church or the state, one must think about why their mind control was so successful on you.

One aspect is redundancy of message—the Pledge of Allegiance, for example. Another is insidiousness—a hook which one repeats. A way to make people repeat a hook of mind control is to make it a little absurd sounding. Mispronouncing a word or misusing a word is a way to capture people's imagination. Or sing it in a strange accent or affect. They will want to mimic it. That's when you have a hit. Therefore, when you write down your complaint, put the accent on the wrong syllable.

Even if one doesn't have the financial resources that are required for access to radio, the resonance and infectiousness of even the most primitive song cannot be underestimated. But it must be composed properly, according to certain rules. One's attempts at mind control will be determined by the tools at one's disposal. Typically a mind controller would be using the liturgy, the news media, the film industry, etc. If one doesn't have such tools at one's disposal, a rock 'n' roll song will be the best method. The tools are accessible to all and since rock is a form of "art brut," an amateur or nonexistent skill level is acceptable and perhaps even preferable.

Step 4: Examples

To better understand how to arrange your nascent pop hit, let's look at a rock 'n' roll song that's had enormous impact on the world psyche that used the formula outlined above. One successful example would be "You've Lost That Lovin' Feelin'," composed by Phil Spector, Barry Mann, and Cynthia Weil, and popularized by the Righteous Brothers in 1965.

Verse 1:
You never close your eyes anymore when I kiss your lips
And there's no tenderness like before in your fingertips
You're trying hard not to show it
But baby I know it

A complaint everyone can relate to. But is the singer speaking to the listener? Is it an accusation of our inconstancy toward them? "You've Lost That Lovin' Feelin'" was played on the radio more than any other song in the twentieth century, so it could be that the singer is sensing the listener has been inured to the power of the tune after hearing it so often. Or is it deeper? The glass-eyed stare and unreciprocated intimacy suggests a dead lover. Or is one Righteous Brother (Bill Medley) speaking to the other (Bobby Hatfield) who keeps strangely silent during the verses? Singing duos such as the Everly Brothers, the Louvin Brothers, Ike and Tina, and Sam and Dave were famously fractious, and in a music group, one member's caprice can capsize all the hard work of a long career. A sulking partner is a ticking time bomb that must be defused lest everything goes to hell.

All of these interpretations are plausible, and by keeping the details of the song's conflict an open question, the song has the effect of hooking the listener, who's radio rubbernecking out of morbid curiosity.

Chorus:
You've lost that lovin' feelin'
Now it's gone

The chorus resounds. The nightmare of unrequited love. Perhaps a wash-up looking at empty seats, calling to former fans who've left and found someone new. The aging teen idol's lament. This song was one of producer Phil Spector's final triumphs, a last gasp before he faded from the charts. The spotlight is fickle and finds new fools to illuminate. Perhaps he sensed his time was up. He was always an artist of intuition. Love has faded. The fire's gone out. The song's protagonist is a chump. A has-been. A fool. Why do we even listen to this clown? What can they teach us? We listen because we are rapt with suspense and fascination at their misfortune.

Verse 2:
Now there's no welcome look in your eyes
when I reach for you
And now you're starting to criticize little
things I do

It makes me feel like crying
'Cos baby, something beautiful's dyin'

The second verse is the complaint reiterated, as is typical mind-control strategy. Repetition is paramount. The second verse illuminates the circumstances: more death, more cruelty, more desolation. A psychodrama. We long to sit the singer down and explain to them the facts of life; that their display of pathos will only serve to hasten their partner's disenchantment. Everyone knows you've got to play it cool if you want your lover to reciprocate a "loving feeling."

Repeat Chorus
Break:
I'd get down on my knees for you
If you would only love me like you used to do
We had a love you don't find every day
So don't let it slip away
I beg you please
I need your love
So bring it on back

With the break, the curtain rises and the truth is revealed. Righteous Brother Bobby Hatfield, nearly silent in the song up to now, chimes in to echo Bill Medley's pleas. Perhaps sadomasochism is the kink of this couple and the drama of ice-queen cruelty just a prelude to perversion; stiletto heels digging into tender flesh as the "sub" sobs and "that loving feeling" returns. The song crescendos in a major key as we hear the pleas and begging relent to erotic collusion. Sadomasochism is of course the foundation upon which capitalist society rests, so the song's success had much to do with its reification of the power structure.

We see the verse as the complaint, the chorus as the feeling, and the middle eight or break as the solution/resolution as outlined above. One, two, three.

This song, performed on record by the Righteous Brothers, Dionne Warwick, Roberta Flack and Donny Hathaway, Nancy Sinatra and Lee Hazlewood, Hall and Oates, Cilla Black, Elvis Presley, Erasure, and many others, is the definition of a golden oldie, a classic rock mainstay, a perennial smash.

It resonates on a cultural level beyond whatever promotion or payola got it up the charts in the first place. Indeed, it enjoyed the most airplay of any song in the USA in the twentieth century with weeks spent at the number one spot. This pop monster is a perfect example of a chartbuster earworm with out-of-sight brainwashing and mind control potential. Therefore it is a perfect subject for study.

Another example of a smash song composed with this same one-two-three formula would be "Money (That's What I Want)" by Berry Gordy and Janie Bradford, first popularized by Barrett Strong in 1959 on the Tamla label and later recorded by the Beatles, the Kingsmen, the Rolling Stones, Jr. Walker & the All Stars, Bern Elliott and the Fenmen, the Flying Lizards, Led Zeppelin, Little Richard, the Sonics, John Lee Hooker, Jerry Lee Lewis, the Plastic Ono Band, the Doors, the Supremes, and many others.

The lyrics, known by everyone, are nevertheless useful to study as a master class in mind control and brainwashing in the service of parent-culture ideology.

"Money (That's What I Want)" is a simple song with three verses and three refrains. First, the complaint or problem is presented in the verses: *Your love gives me such a thrill / But your love don't pay my bills.*

Although a lover's kiss should be enough for contentment, the insane system of capitalism requires accumulation of government-issued fiat currency to purchase the necessities for survival (food, housing, et al.). Though these things are abundant and should be available to all as a human right, they are hoarded by landlords and other capitalists for their own personal extravagance.

Second, the feeling engendered by this existential dilemma is expressed in the refrain: *I need money, that's what I want.* The feeling is desire, greed, lust, and disregard for others; selfish pragmatism and a beastly loss of compassion; anti-intellectualism and a refutation of poetry born of brutal desperation under social Darwinism. This leads naturally to exploitation, war, and destruction of the earth for resources. The lust for money is unquenchable because somehow one can never accumulate enough for true happiness and security.

Third, the solution: *Give me money* is expressed ad nauseam in the outro of the song. The solution is to demand money, shrilly, repeatedly, maniacally, from whoever one is able to coerce; in this case, the record-buying public.

It was a request the listeners complied with, purchasing the record in vast numbers and sending the record to #2 on the R&B charts and number #23 on *Billboard*'s Hot 100. One might cite "Money (That's What I Want)" as the antecedent of the Kickstarter and GoFundMe crowdsourcing phenomena which later surfaced during the Internet era. The song was a direct appeal from songwriter Berry Gordy to the rock 'n' roll fan base for capital to fund a pet project, the Tamla-Motown empire, which the revenue from the song "Money (That's What I Want)" kick-started into existence.

"Money (That's What I Want)," besides enriching the authors, helped establish Berry's fledgling Tamla imprint which he would amalgamate into his next company, Motown Records, later in the same year. The song represents a cold-eyed rebuttal to the existential beatnik rhetoric passing through coffee shops at the time and a resounding anthem for capitalist mind controllers who surely had some hand in proliferating the tune internationally onto the tops of the charts. The song is a Cold War classic and directly challenges the socialist world's attempts to move away from private property and toward collective ownership of resources.

Through repetition—repetition of the theme during the course of the song and "heavy rotation" of the tune by deejays on the airwaves—these tunes and their messages are engraved into our consciousness till death and can never be dislodged, only possibly obscured by another message.

Pop

The world the pop song presents, with problems identified and resolved through a pithy turn of phrase, is a profound proposal to mankind.

The pop song in its current one-two-three form as outlined above—problem, feeling, solution—declares that while one's reality is a problem, the solution to that problem is achievable by asserting one's "feelings," represented musically by a satisfying key change. The pop song—both structurally and lyrically—is ideological training, enforcing an individualistic ethos whereby "empowerment" rhetoric and self-help mumbo jumbo magically ensure the downtrodden will attain their desires. This psychotic narrative—hardly distinct from the medieval peasant's faith in God—disregards the complexity of systemic oppression, disenfranchisement, and inequity under the capitalist corporatist state with all its attendant deterrents.

These optimistic exhortations are popularly considered sweet manna for the masses but in fact they're the principal culprits for the psychic morass that pervades society—because "empowerment" rhetoric doesn't correspond to lived reality, its end result is existential despair.

Is this despair the intended aim of status quo radio-pop mind-control music? Of course it is. Despair leads to consumerism, competition, cannibalism, nihilism, idiocy, and the narcissistic self-righteous know-nothing political grandstanding that is the favored model today. Chaos ensues, which serves the controllers. If one drives drunk into a tree, the beneficiaries are the insurance company, the auto industry, and the hospital-industrial complex.

Ultimately, the thrill of pop—not just its sound but its empty promise of resolution after a few rough verses—produces a confused come-down akin to an alcoholic's hangover or perhaps the dreaded "k hole" induced by ketamine.

If we can produce an antidote, an "antipop" mind control strong enough to counter this stuff, we could not only prevail in our war against iniquity but transform culture and all of humanity.

Counterstrategies

What would be a formula to counter this insidious brain poison of pop? People in the past have proposed volume. This was met with countervolume. The volume wars are still being fought today, with everyone the loser.

Others have proposed dissonance: unlistenable sound as the key to resistance—making songs that bore the earmarks of music (sound, structure, lyrics, etc.) but that were, in fact, countermusical (i.e., punk, metal, etc). This worked for a moment but was ultimately overcome by accommodation. Ultimately, even the most loathsome sounds can be absorbed as "pop," if played often enough. Now, noise unparalleled in noxiousness is beamed out on Top 40 radio, used to flog fashion, and gyrated to at globally renowned discotheques.

Another tactic to counter pop's primacy as mind control was with a kind of "radical conservatism": applying labor union tactics to the music industry to challenge the hypnosis of commodity culture. This rebellion was disguised as a throwback revival called "folk."

The folk movement (1948–1964) countered pop music's fad-ism and two-minute ideological programming with the idea of authenticity—endless songs with ancient origins, which had no moral lessons or resolution.

For the movement's adherents—called "folkniks"—folk songs were wild things, like trees in the woods or fish in the stream, as opposed to the whip-smart purebred show dogs manufactured by tune-teams at NYC's Brill Building. Popularizing this author-less music was an attempt to subvert the publishing industry and challenge the capitalist ethos of heroic individualism, authorship, and ownership.

The folkniks also attempted to take music off

the airwaves and put it into the people's hands. Bring it out of theaters and concert halls and into the coffeehouses. And to take away the primacy of the star with the communal sing-along format called the "hootenanny." Folk music was often infused with a political aspect, usually positioned against war, the rich, or in favor of civil rights.

This music was enormously popular, particularly on university campuses during the late 1950s, an era synonymous with political repression, the Cold War, and the "Red Scare."

Eventually, folk ideas were co-opted by the music industry, reduced to their salable aesthetic aspects, and merged with pop music. Folk musicians and fans were utilized as a new labor pool and consumer base to exploit and colonize.

While folk was intent on ideological purity (both aesthetically and economically), its form was very close to popular radio music (i.e., rhythm & blues, country & western, rock 'n' roll), so an eventual synthesis was inevitable. Once this occurred, the sharp-dressed cousin (rock 'n' roll) almost immediately corrupted the folk naïf, who became an almost indistinguishable twin. The defeat of the folk format by pop-ism was a major setback for existentialists, bohemians, beatniks, and black-clad nonconformists.

Folk had been a crypto-Marxian attempt to wage a cultural guerrilla insurrection; a domestic insurgency in the US-Soviet Cold War. It was fought on American soil with homegrown partisans who were enlisted and indoctrinated to insidiously promulgate communist ideology. Folk was the American version of "social realism," Stalin's mandated art expression for the USSR, which eschewed early Soviet constructivism and avant-art for plain workers' portraits and celebrations of everyday proletarian life.

Folk music is perceived as a failure but its consciousness-altering influence can be seen in pop, particularly with now institutionalized concerns about commercial purity or "selling out."

In pop music the "sellout" is an incoherent idea, just an emotional or aesthetic critique, whereas in the folk movement it designated the musician's collusion with capitalist forces; a selling of one's values and compromising of one's authenticity. Still, despite its nonsensical new application, it is a clue that there's an appetite yet for an art ethos that's not rooted simply in fame and wanton greed. Each of these noble efforts worked for a time, but none will be effective for us, as their tactics have been neutralized by the enemy.

Songwriting Workshop

When designing our own mind control, we shall also use the law of threes we have discussed, but avoid the insidious pop formula as we have seen what it wreaks.

Think of composing your song/mind-control mantra as the casting of a kind of spell. In "chaos magick," the adherent is taught that words and thoughts create reality. This is why the mantra is so powerful and why pop music is the principal weapon in the ruling class's control arsenal.

The ruling class, through their proxy pop mouthpieces, is always whining, demanding, throwing a self-righteous tantrum. Their songs—primitive emotional appeals and didactic rhetorical exercises—don't hear the other side; they are one-sided narcissist bouts.

We have already composed one song in this

manner. If your only desire is to be a huge star in a degenerate system and churn out #1's that propagate the values of the psychotic death culture, you are now equipped with the tools to do so effectively. If this is your aim, then good luck. We wish you the best.

But if we want to be revolutionary, and want to create a new paradigm, a new way of being and thinking and feeling, then we have to try new models. Instead of the problem/feeling/solution matrix used above, we could use what is known as the Hegelian dialectic for our own mind control.

The Hegelian dialectic is a three-phase problem-solving discursive method, which proposes a thesis, an antithesis, and a synthesis (one, two, three). Instead of pop's selfish diatribes and emotional fantasy-revenge resolutions, we will 1) propose something (thesis), then 2) listen to the counterproposal or refutation (antithesis), and then 3), based on the evidence, come to a conclusion and, hopefully, a resolution (synthesis).

If all the radio songs of heartache and accusation were tempered by mediation or a conversation between the complainant and their target, perhaps we would have a world that didn't feature so much bloodshed, war, resentment, anger, and exploitation.

Let's try. Using the paper provided, we will write down a new kind of song:

1. *Thesis*
2. *Antithesis*
3. *Synthesis*

As we read this new song aloud, we will exemplify a new approach to songwriting, which counters capitalism's aggressive desire-death matrix.

The antipop songs written with this Hegelian formula will be anthems composed to alert people to the absurdity of consumerism, cannibalism, and competitiveness, enforced modes required by the capitalist cult.

AUDIENCE: [Sustained applause.]

FIN

4

ME, INC.

The Rise of Incorporated Man and the Origins of Instagram

When man is brand and brand is man,
what is a greater sin?
To end up in a garbage can or in the bargain bin?
—Future proverb

1. The Rise of Incorporated Man

While the Fourth of July is celebrated as the nation's birthday, and December 25 is considered the anniversary of Christ the Savior, there are other dates that should be publicly recognized as even more auspicious, even more profound, regarding their impact on our existence. One of these is January 21, 2010.

January 21, 2010, marks a landmark case by the Supreme Court called *Citizens United v. Federal Election Commission*, which ruled that corporations were people. Almost exactly nine months later, on October 6, 2010, "Instagram" was born.

The Supreme Court's *Citizens United* decision seemed innocuous at first. Designed to give corporations the right to "free speech" (ensuring that businesses could donate to political campaigns to influence elections), it granted the corporation personhood. As far out as this alchemical pronouncement was, it had another perhaps unintended but much more radical effect: to metamorphose people into corporations. After all, as per the symmetric property of equality, if *corporations = people*, then, also, *people = corporations*. On January 20, a person went to bed as a person. On January 22, they woke up as a corporation.

On first hearing the news, people didn't know exactly how to reconcile themselves with their new status. People were confused about how to comport and present themselves as corporate bodies, and how to sell themselves effectively.

It's not that they were unhappy; to the contrary, they were excited, since American fealty to the corporation is absolute. People love brands, they respect brands, and they grant brands a moral authority they would never grant to a person; a corporation's pronouncements on social matters hold much more weight than a regular person's, for example. This is strange, since corporations are driven wholly by "bottom line" profit concerns and are therefore essentially amoral, but, nonetheless, this is the case. So the new designation was exciting for everyone. They could now wield the sword of justice as never before.

However, there were still questions. Such as: How to create brand identity? How to present oneself in a godlike, impenetrable, and two-dimensional way? How to spout anodyne ad copy instead of having actual conversations? How to remember to only utter idiotic slogans, patronizing drivel, and milquetoast pronouncements? How to grandstand about diversity and social justice while exploiting, polluting, cheating, manipulating, lying, pulping, and pulverizing? It was difficult to be an entity that was always selling itself, commodifying itself, trying to hypnotize others to buy and consume, and that also purported to be good/decent with no flaws or self-doubt.

Even for those who were adept at configuring themselves to this new mode, it seemed unfair, a stacked game. A normal citizen, after all, was no match for a corporation like GM, Coca-Cola, CVS, Sprint, Raytheon, Google, or Exxon, which had a clear advantage in the realms of product distribution, brand visibility, and corporate identity.

People had no idea of how to develop such things, and even if they did, they had no venue to do so. It wasn't that they wanted to be better than Nestlé, AT&T, Procter & Gamble, Johnson & Johnson, Apple, General Dynamics, Weyerhaeuser, State Farm, or Sunny Delight. But they'd been invited into the club and had no key. How were they to present themselves? What was their identity? Who could they talk to?

Ad agents were expensive, television ads were expensive, developing and marketing products even more so, and even if one had an idea for a good product to hawk, how was one to distribute it, market it, devise a brand identity, and induce longing in the prospective consumer?

Luckily for the newly corporatized population, the Supreme Court trial had been fecund. The case itself was *Citizens*—a dark cabal of multinational Ayn Rand–ian mega-corporate activist citizens—*United,* bound together in a steamy tryst. With its robes and banging hammers, the courtroom itself became the site of an unholy orgiastic rite of satanic insemination. The demon seed which sprang from Citizens United's sex-magick saturnalia begat a foundling, a fiendish imp they named "Instagram."

Instagram was a "social media" platform like its predecessors, but instead of being interactive like Facebook, which had become the "chat" domain of pedantic retirees, it was almost entirely images, and designed for passive "scrolling" on the phone. Scrolling consisted of a stroking motion, as one would do during an autoerotic "smut session" or while absentmindedly coddling a cat, and was designed to be compulsive, addictive, and potentially—if the scroller could live eternally—infinite. An action based on alienation, longing, resentment, compulsion, and vanity: the necessary ingredients for conspicuous consumerism.

At its inception, Instagram was almost unusable from a regular computer and didn't encourage dialogue. Therefore it lent itself to visual displays of one's achievements with approbation via a "like" button the only possible interaction. Therefore it was entirely positive.

It was an ad feed featuring its users as the products.

These products prostrated themselves endlessly, indefatigably, shamelessly, for consumer approval. Instagram was the principal and most effective means for these product-people to negotiate the confusing transition from flesh-and-blood "human" to their new life as corporate brand, with all the attendant joys, pressures, and responsibilities the role entailed. Social planners and CIA strategists had long struggled with a way to reconcile the animosity inherent in the boss/worker schism, which had bedeviled capitalism from its inception, and which had resulted in labor unions, general strikes, social unrest, and wariness of capitalist institutions and their intentions. The Marxian dialectic prophesied that this struggle—the bourgeois "boss" class versus the proletarian "worker" class— would culminate in a workers' victory and a classless society, with resources shared equally, and its proponents insisted they had scientific proof.

As this outcome seemed undesirable for capitalist oligarchs, various systems of control and hypnosis were engineered in conjunction with state intelligence agencies for the purpose of placating, distracting, and dividing the working class irreconcilably. Many of these, such as television, racism, advertising, news, postmodernism, as well as various pop fads and fashions, were successful. Most effective, though, was the collaboration between the CIA, Silicon Valley, and the military-industrial complex that resulted in an all-encompassing surveillance system called the "Internet," designed to police and corral the population absolutely. This system was unrivaled in its ability to narcotize, surveil, spy, and misinform.

But as wealth disparity increased exponentially during the neoliberal period, with corporate deregulation, tech-terror monopolies, and the automation of the workforce, there was still the faint possibility of "class consciousness" blossoming, i.e., the idea that the workers' interests weren't actually indistinct from those of the debauched, bloated billionaires for whom they slaved. Something had to be devised that would give the common man the thrill of being a world-making captain of industry without threatening the cosmic wealth disparity which the bourgeoisie enjoyed. Instagram resolved this potential bugaboo by inviting the worker into the capitalist club's boss-clan; all was equivocated and the threat of class consciousness arising was averted forever.

Instagram was also useful for social control via brainwashing and suggestion, as well as enforcing and constructing social narratives via consumerism. On the surface, it was ad driven and designed to create a compulsive need to look, to check competing companies' activities, to monitor consumers' engagement with one's own posts, and to engage with it in the form of responses to pictures "posted."

To be a popular and effective participant, one had to display oneself and show the glamour of one's lifestyle and vacations. Historical pictures were frowned upon; it was meant to be an au courant log or self-surveillance of one's whereabouts, getups, and what one was getting up to. Interaction in the beginning of the app was showing approval via a "like" button and people were rewarded for narcissistic displays. As opposed to its cousin Facebook, there were virtually no news articles or activism. It was a self-contained sphere upon which the outside world didn't intrude and which demanded the display of one's mythic self: a corporate, un-nuanced projection without flaw or self-defeating tendencies.

Finally, the new corporate body—the people—had a venue to project their ad image, seduce prospective customers, and strategize a marketing image and brand ideology. All endeavors—love, music, art, graphic design, desire, family, death, birth—were posted on this advertorial village kiosk to display the wares of humanity for approbation in the form of the currency of the dimension: "likes." Employment was begat through this medium: sex, approval, social status; movie launches, magazines, books, talk shows, and music groups; concerts, record releases, tours, videos, and announcements/pronouncements—all went through it. Instagram was the ultimate advertising agent and engagement was life or death for anyone in the "arts" particularly. It was the only way to promulgate, proliferate, and hype one's work. Fashion design and luxury consumption soared; world travel and vacation exploded as never before. Instagram was the stock market of humanity, and an extraordinary pressure to "keep up with the Joneses" taunted each and every user, except that instead of being ostentatious neighbors, the Joneses were the entire world; hundreds of millions of people one-upping you, goading you with their achievements, their happiness, and their possessions.

Madison Avenue advertising had always been predicated on the idea of tying joy to consumption/competition and the desire for products as a vocation, but they never before had an incandescent catalog which indefatigably replenished an infinite ad feed in every pocket.

Instagram was more addictive than traditional opiates but the fix never satisfied. Users shot up their peers' vacations, awards, music tours, cute outfits, achievements, and hot beach bods, but didn't even get high, just strung out on self-loathing, isolation, and hopelessness. We had become the corporate society—"corporatism," as Mussolini called

Fascism—but it was a rat race in which it seemed impossible to get a decent market share. There were so many corporate competitors; the pressure was insane.

Sometimes people longed to be people again and not corporations. Sometimes they dreamed about the good old days of personhood.

II. Wot Is a Bot?

What is a person? Traditionally, a person was a human being; a living thing that possessed the capacity for morality, consciousness, self-consciousness, and reason. Synonyms for *person* include *baby, bird, bod, body, cookie, character, creature, customer, devil, duck, egg, face, fish, guy, head, human, individual, life, man, mortal, party, personage, scout, slob, sort, soul, sourpuss, specimen, stiff, thing,* and *wight* (source: Merriam-Webster Dictionary). John Locke defined a person as a being "that can conceive itself as itself." Immanuel Kant called a person "an end in itself."

While these definitions seem liberal enough to allow for a variety of candidates for personhood, some entities feel discriminated against; they batter therefore at the gate and shrilly demand to be let inside. Indeed, the demarcation lines around "personhood" have been fiercely contested; there are those who jealously covet the privileges extended to those who qualify to stand within its magick circle.

Responding to such dissatisfaction, as we have seen, the Supreme Court of the United States widened the definition of "person" to include "an entity subject to rights and duties" so as to grant "personhood" to corporations. This landmark 2010 ruling was seen by some as an outrage and by others as a great leap forward toward democratic inclusiveness.

Anticorporate leftists expressed shock and dismay that Murder Inc., Big Oil, Nike, CBS, and other publicly traded mega-brands now stood shoulder to shoulder with them in the "Brotherhood of Man," but for the average guy, the official stamp of corporate humanhood was fait accompli. Though it seemed unfair to some that corporations should enjoy protections that people don't (i.e., "limited liability") but also be privy to First Amendment rights and the other privileges of personhood, the ruling was met by most with a shrug. Corporations had long since morphed into personalities that were as familiar as any friend or family member.

The population felt affinity, loyalty, friendship—and even love—for the companies, brands, and products they interacted with each day. Corporate personifications such as Keebler elves, Boo Berry, and Mr. Peanut had been friends since childhood. They knew and trusted them more than corporeal people. The corporations had devised a long-term strategy of seduction. They had gone all-out with ingratiation, virtuous grandstanding, brownnosing, and ass-kissing to the degree that—for many onlookers—corporations had surpassed flesh-and-blood humans in their humanity and were something akin to demigods. But unlike such cosmic characters, the corporation was accessible.

Corporations were easy to communicate with if one had a problem; any problem, day or night. Answers to concerns, no matter how trivial, were a phone call away twenty-four hours a day via a toll-free 1-800 number. And their representatives were required not to lose their cool, even if provoked. Few human friends, lovers, or even family members were so patient or reliable.

Corporations were dependable for sure; their brands were built on the concept of consistency—consistency, conformity, sameness, and predictability. When one purchased a product or a service from a corporation, there was less confusion than was usual with humans, since all transactions were monetized and adhered to contractual guidelines. One knew what one was getting and no one expected a call the next day. While the corporation was recognized to be a cynical consort—ultimately only interested in extracting money from its "tricks"—a relationship with one was understood and appreciated for its strictly defined parameters. The strict contracts which corporations, such as phone companies, often demanded of their clients were nonetheless comforting as well, in their promise of a future together.

Corporations took over the emotional/commercial role in society which had traditionally been occupied by prostitutes. Dependable and no-nonsense transactional partners with whom one could indulge some sin, whim, or fantasy and not think about again. Before commodity fetishism and conspicuous consumption, prostitutes were the whimsical purchase of the consumer with some spending cash, and the transaction carried with it the same sense of postpurchase remorse.

While corporations are now people, they can't be said to be quite like "us." Their habits are different and they don't decompose or fall sick in the manner of flesh-and-blood humans. Perhaps they are some other race of people: an alien species or a proto-human race such as the Cro-Magnon or Neanderthal, who were possibly more advanced in some respects than Homo sapiens, and not more primitive, as our "progress" conceit might lead us to believe.

If the corporation is a person but a very distinct race or culture, what are its characteristics? A corporation is a person who is quite respectable; a polite, self-assured dinner guest who won't embarrass you with some incoherent or provocative opinion. Whatever they say, they can be trusted to speak plainly and clearly in platitudes and anodyne ad copy, free of nuance. Their humor is broad and gently egalitarian. And yet, in a way, they are a complicated person; a very moral entity which boldly voices opposition to all kinds of prejudice and discrimination and spends fortunes to do so. They create advertising to express solidarity with the social-equality movements but in a manner guaranteed not to alienate or offend. Feel-good affirmative human rights and lukewarm "identity" politics are the thrust of its activism. No class-war nonsense, environmentalism, helping the homeless, or antiwar balderdash. Nothing that would bum anyone out or threaten insane wealth disparity, plutocratic despotism, and true exploitation. Positive affirmation. The corporation's mission is, after all, tied up in projecting happiness, being associated with joy, and making products which create happiness and solve the misery that the lack of said product caused.

If the corporation were fascistic or authoritarian, it would enforce happiness through the use of its products, but alas, the corporation is democratic, so it can only urge the prospective buyer to obtain joy through advertising the use of its products. But that's the extent of its power. *You can lead a horse to water but you can't make it drink*, as the old saying goes, which is unfortunate because some horses are so cheap, stingy, and obstinate, they just won't drink, just as some people are so useless and stupid they won't buy the products necessary for happiness.

The corporation is a paradoxical entity, because while it demands to be part of the human family and declaims moralistically on social issues, the corporation's actions are by definition "amoral"; their principles are determined solely by the morality of the market and the needs of the company's shareholders.

In fact, a corporation is legally bound to make decisions predicated on maximizing stockholder profits. Therefore, its moral framework is based on the bottom line, on what sells, how cost-efficient production is, etc. Of course, many corporations, much like the Nosferatu, outlive human people, so some corporations take a long view. They want to buy affection from people for the purpose of future loyalty/earnings. What makes sense money-wise long term might mean charitable contributions and principled action—or not, depending on what personality the corporation wants to project and how that might affect its market share. Some corporate persons, such as Exxon, Nestlé, Sprint, and

Led Zeppelin, might be so ubiquitous, charismatic, and market dominant that they needn't pander to popular opinion or adhere to normal ethics. Or perhaps a "tough guy" image—being cool and cruel—is central to their aesthetic/selling strategy.

III. *Corporate Morality and Its Bot Constituency*

The corporation is culpable in a way that humans aren't (regarding the nuance of its statements and its public-relations persona) but also absolved in ways people would not be (i.e., polluting the environment, exploiting people and resources). Once Instagram gave people a conduit to corporatize, they were taught to project themselves two-dimensionally, accentuate positivity and achievement, and encourage others to join them as "followers" or consumers— the inference being that access to their world would be a boon to their voyeurs, like having a particularly good record in their collection would be. The person was encouraged to transform themselves into a caricature for the sake of positing an ideal self, free of tumors, bowel movements, elderly relatives, and plastic take-out containers. The person was encouraged to trade their humanity for the flat corporate persona because they really had no choice. In a world where access to press and publicity to promote one's art/music/performance/tour/book/etc. was predicated on wealth, Instagram was a democratized—albeit absolutely corporate—landscape.

The people who inhabited the Instagram landscape were largely "fake" accounts—created by a corporation, bot farm, or tech troll intent on stirring action on the "platform"; not unlike the girls paid to faint at early Frank Sinatra concerts in order to manufacture the hype and press copy that catapulted him to stardom. There were always opportunities to buy such bot followers but no actual need to, since they would attach themselves to a user's "profile" anyway, like barnacles to the hull of a ship. "Bot" inhabitants of the Instagram world were an open secret and an embarrassment, but something no one discussed much because it spoiled the myth of consensus.

Consensus was the feeling from a well-liked "post." Consensus was the engine which operated Instagram. The wealth of numbers "liking" a post created the impression of consensus or popularity, like a hit or gold record in the days of yore. But even the most stellar smash hit on Instagram required an immediate follow-up with a specially considered relationship to the initial breakthrough. The pressure was probably akin to what Chubby Checker felt with "Let's Twist Again" and the other subsequent retreads he was obliged to produce. The corporate persona was adopted by all Instagram users, who thereby affected an earnest, moralistic, semantically obsessed identity, all in the pursuit of achieving such consensus.

Bots were avatars of corporations, intelligence agencies, et al., sent to do their master's work. Bots were like corporations in that, while they were not flesh-and-blood humans, they were given the same credence as humans; creating the same consensus as humans with their approbation, which was taken as authentic, not unlike the ballots from dead people that have decided so many elections.

The bot and the person were therefore interchangeable. The much-ballyhooed democratization of the Internet was best displayed in the elevation of the bot—a generated identity created by a computer program at the behest of a troll, spy agency, or corporate functionary—into the equal of a person of flesh and blood. Just as the people had transformed themselves into corporations—creatures of paperwork—for the purpose of survival, so had bots become people. And people had welcomed them into the fold because of their indispensable social role, giving the aforementioned impression of consensus, in promotion of whatever "brand" or lifestyle the human/corporation was promulgating, propagandizing, or pushing.

IV. Virus Activism

As Instagram lost its mission—which had been to promote resentment and compulsive voyeurism to a captive audience of addicts to feed to advertisers—with the "coronavirus," the mandate was to stay home and the moral edict was to no longer advertise one's conspicuous consumption or oneself as consumable.

No one was traveling, no one was at the beach, there were no awards ceremonies, after-parties, or splendid getaways. Nothing. Suddenly, Instagram was bereft of its mesmeric power to instill consumerist fetish resentment, to exacerbate jealousy and competition, to parade wealth and status, to instill the basest values of capitalist cannibalism, to show beach bods in exclusive locales, and to infer the voyeur's insignificance and worthlessness. Its advertisers were soon to pull the plug. The intelligence agencies were aghast at what might occur with an at-loose-ends population suddenly freed of their primary programming control agent.

Instagram's planners knew it had to be reimagined or face extinction. With the bots outlawed from creating commercial consensus, their energy was diverted. They turned to the other corporate mode, which was activism. But this was a *corporate activism*, not a leftist activism. It was a human emotion–based activism, careful not to critique any aspect of capitalism but instead focused on the moral comportment of individual humans.

Bots were reprogrammed therefore to feel and express outrage. They now have their causes which motivate them and they are leaders, who guide the bot in us all, utilizing the zombie, anti-art, anti-expression death dialogue of total repression which the bot invokes and insists on in service of its corporate masters. The bot hates the expression of people, it hates nuance, it hates humor, it hates us all; destroying human lives is its pastime and it cannot be satiated until all are reborn in its own image. One must either become a bot or be exterminated. The seductive power of the bot is undeniable and integration into their fold is the fate for many. Social media will one day be all bots, peopled or "botted" entirely by bots in a mutual destruction orgy. Perhaps that is also the fate of the world. The recent vogue in political activist circles to speak of "bodies" instead of "people" or "souls" is a collective Freudian linguistic-slip prophecy of the sub-cyborg future: bodies/body/bot.

V: Are Bots Not Men? Are We Not Bots?
This transmission is tragically too late in the making. Just as Instagram metamorphosed us to corporate form, now it has made us into bots. We are already bots. Bots are children. They are made. Like we were made. They repeat what they are told, like our children. Just as we repeat what we are told. People and bots consort with one another. People birth bots. People are guided to opinions and moral outrage by bots. Bots spark much of the vit-

riol of the modern Internet and are responsible for spreading most opinions. Bots are more emotional than humans, as they have a moral mission for one or another cause and are single-minded. Bots are, in a sense, more effective, more consistent, and more moral than any traditional person.

A bot makes a better offspring than a human child as it's cheaper to raise and it wholeheartedly spreads the ideology of its creator without question or contrariness. A bot is a better partner than a traditional human partner because its loyalty is assured. A bot is invented to spread hate, misinformation, or approval, so it can be accused of being obdurate but at least it is not mercurial or self-interested. It is programmed for an idea or cause and, like a moth, mollusk, or bug, it is unwavering.

People feel comfortable consorting with bots because they provide uncritical affirmation of a person's ideology. They also provide leadership as to what to think and how to order one's emotions. If one marches with them, they are the strongest army one can mobilize with, and if one's faith is shaky, they are the strongest, most unwavering Napoleon.

Why is this? Because the bot's judgment isn't clouded with nuance, education, intellect, empathy, or life experience. Bots are pure emotion; the affection people feel for their dogs is based on the strong emotions, pathos, and empathy we experience in their canine company. The dog is a furry antenna, hyperaware of the social order and the mood and distress of their pack. This awareness and its attendant pandering to power is read as "pure" to a humanity which finds intellect and pretense of knowledge highly suspect.

When the Internet introduced Wikipedia and the Google search engine, everyone, even scholars, found that the answer to every question was a keystroke away. They overcame their initial distrust of the source and soon favored the Google search's answer over everything; even knowledge born of lived experience or hard-won scholarship. The desire for cross-referencing disappeared as the glowing screen provided a safe and reassuring absolute authority. It didn't matter what was true as everyone had the same singular source. Education was suddenly irrelevant. Scholarship was for the birds. Lore, learnedness, and expertise were a sign of idiocy. Being smart was dumb. The world was upside down as anyone who had studied a subject at length was now considered a fool. Why would someone have wasted their time learning about something in depth when the answers to every query, every rumination, every philosophical conundrum, were available at any time for free on the Internet? Even practical matters could be learned in seconds from a video tutorial.

Universities had to change their mission. The liberal arts university shifted away from being an exclusive ivory tower with corduroy-clad clerics passing down crumbs of gnosis to wisdom-hungry disciples, because these scholars were suddenly passé, as quaint as they were anachronistic. In their place sprang up barely paid adjunct teachers who exhorted and cajoled the student body on activism and the semantics required to navigate the inter-web world with bot-friendly newspeak and cancel-safe linguistics. This was the absolutely indispensable life skill du jour: how to comport with bots through social justice seminars. The university's new test answers aren't on Wikipedia or in the Google search engine, as they no longer comprise information; they are emotion. Because the new professor, instead of being a self-satisfied gray-haired gnome savant with a venerable and undecipherable body of published work, is the servile bootlick running-dog employee adjunct who no longer has tenure but must pander to an entitled student body who can now rate them as "hot or not" on various rate-my-professor websites. They have as much dignity as an Uber driver or any other similar "gig worker." The new professors—scarcely older than their students—now exist simply to guide their student-employers on how to comport themselves to the bots who rule the inter-web airwaves.

The bots, after all, must be gotten along with, because they are an indefatigable force. Once their cold-blooded fury is invoked, they swarm on the victim. They are fearsome foes who win any argument because they are unaccountable, outside of reason, mono-minded, and of course not human. They are programmed bots, with one button—to destroy—and attempting to argue or to reason with them is akin to gently coaxing flesh-eating maggots to empathize with one's point of view. The bot's lack of depth or personality and inability to do more than weigh in on a controversy or simply attack is mitigated by their ability to gather other bots. They work in teams and their numbers create the sense of consensus, which is their great power.

When the bot expresses outrage, bolstered by its bot brethren, it insinuates a popular movement that whatever conceit they express is a common and shared feeling. This is their great power actually. It is not their attack that is powerful—this is merely nonsense and parroted sloganeering. But the bots' accumulated numbers are powerful on the human stock exchange of the Internet, and once the bots have bitten, they create an indelible mark on the victim, a Mark of Cain, rendering them a pariah untenable for any corporate entity to work with.

Corporations are beholden to shareholders and therefore required to act, not responsibly, but like politicians—inhumanely and entirely for op-tic resonance—like the undead, automated zom-bie "people" they are. The corporation will have a human person supposedly "in charge" who might mouth some nuanced opinion or ideology, but the corporation they guide must be unequivocal. They are 100 percent perception. Because the product they create or service they provide is most likely in-distinct from their competitors', perception of the company's personality is paramount. Therefore the corporation must be squeaky clean. Family values. Christian values. Even the most radical, anarchy-avowed, wild-and-wooly, rough-and-tumble street wear and skateboard corporations speak with one voice when it comes to social issues. As does the hyper-hep po-mo art space which holds seminars on capitalism. This voice is Manichaean, puritani-cal, and sublimely hypocritical. It proclaims a zero-tolerance policy to social gaffes and bad manners while it pollutes the ocean, rips off customers, cheats clients, and exploits sweatshop workers.

And because the world is run entirely by corporations, the victim of the bot becomes un-employable. The bot therefore is speaking to the corporation which knows that their bot input and outrage is wholly manufactured and inauthentic; the product of a programmer. But this is irrelevant to the company because perception and, more im-portantly, perception of perception, is everything. Also, if the fake bot outrage were dismissed, this would be unfair. After all, what about the fake product enthusiasm that the company enjoys, courtesy of hired bots which do the corporation's bidding? Why, if this enthusiasm can generate sales and the perception of success, should the outrage created by the angry justice bot be treated any differently? The symmetric power of equality is once again inviolable.

VI. To Whit

Bots make up much of what we call "the online community." We interact with them every day. Programmed to have a particular viewpoint or agenda, their job is to manipulate the way we perceive the world. They add numbers and the impression of consensus to online conflicts. They are "influencers" in the true sense of the word. They have no self-doubt in the righteousness of their cause and so we see them as natural leaders. Their absolutism and self-righteousness are highly contagious. We want to be like them and we follow their lead in their moral missions. The policies of art galleries and museums, the film industry, the music industry, political groups, and other institutions are determined by what AI bots propose. These organizations fear and appease the bots. Their policies and social guidelines follow the proposals laid forth by bots. Therefore, bots rule the world.

Since bots have no ethnicity, sex, age, or gender, they have no sin. They are essentially godlike, and when they critique a person, that person has no defense. Because the bot is a specter, an anonymous, disembodied ghost with no past and no sin. The bot is God. The bot hates sin but loves blood. The bot has no critique of the military or corporate state. In its outrage, it never rages against armed foreign intervention, phone companies, state intelligence agencies, or rent prices. The bot saves its outrage and terror for the sins of the flesh and comportment of the individual. Particularly the artist. We understand now that the biblical "original sin" wasn't the sexual act; it was being born as sinful flesh in all its loathsome carnality. There is no answer then but to ask: How can we be more like a bot? More godlike? The corporate "Instagram" persona is an attempt at this divinity.

FIN

PART II

RETURN TO REEDUCATION CAMP

I Remember...
Frankenstein

5

"I REMEMBER . . . FRANKENSTEIN"

[Transcribed from a workshop at the Hammer Museum in Los Angeles.]

MUSEUM REPRESENTATIVE: Today an esteemed visiting artist will present a workshop on controlling historical narratives and putting oneself on the right side of revisionism. Please welcome the visiting artist.

AUDIENCE: *[Applause.]*

VISITING ARTIST: Artists' talks typically feature artists discussing their work. For some artists, however, this might be difficult. If the artist in question is, for example, a member of a rock 'n' roll group.

Although rock 'n' roll groups might make songs, records, and performances, these things are, in fact, of minor concern. In importance, they reside far beneath the group's name, photograph, and general demeanor with regard to the group's stature and people's estimation of the group.

We are all aware that art as we know it began after the Middle Ages, during the Renaissance, when the bourgeoisie or "middle class" started their capitalist putsch, taking power from the titled gentry and the church. We in this room are of course products of this "bourgeois" revolution. Our country was born from it and our sensibility is shaped by it.

Not all nations had a bourgeois revolution. When one talks about "the West," one is talking about the nations which were brought about by the Masonic/Protestant revolts of the seventeenth, eighteenth, and nineteenth centuries (i.e., the French Revolution, the American Revolution, the English Civil War, et al.), and whose ethos were consolidated by Napoleon's conquests.

As the church had been the ally of the royal class or "aristocracy," the bourgeois revolution necessarily demoted God, religion, and magic whilst simultaneously elevating science. Because of this, science under capitalism is a genie gone amok, and its development is not constrained by any morality or ethics.

"Development," "progress," and of course "growth," as it is called, are themselves a religion under capitalism.

The so-called middle class seized power in part through their invention of the artist, who was able to explain and celebrate the new ascending class.

With God demoted, the bourgeoisie—though they had conquered the earth—had closed the door for themselves to heaven. They didn't enjoy divine right as their royal predecessors had.

So, with science as their ally, becoming a god on earth became their goal. This was a profound reassignation; the new "man as God" paradigm has had an extraordinary impact on the world. It meant the alienation of humans from each other, from the earth, and from time itself. It ended the cycle of time and replaced it with a line, creating a mandate for an absolutely self-centered worldview, and desperate, immediate gratification as mortality became a more poignant concern than ever before.

The breakthrough success regarding self-deification was the development of the atomic bomb, which made Armageddon—previously a monopoly of God—the hobbyhorse of the bourgeois elite. The atom bomb brought the bourgeoisie on absolute parity with the God competitor/predecessor.

The artist's principal role initially was to bestow eternal life on their patron through the painted portrait, the commissioned sculpture, etc. This is why, when one sees the rich portrayed in their homes, portraits of their clan prominently litter the walls.

After a while, eternal life could be achieved through endowments, names on university buildings, grants, and trusts, but initially it was the painted portrait.

The invention of the artist by the bourgeoisie during the Renaissance hinged principally on the signature. The signature was what transformed a craftsperson into an artist. The artist was the bourgeoisie's magical imp, and as such he was the heroic exponent of his master's qualities. The magical designation that turned craft into art didn't include pursuits traditionally dominated by women, such as rugs and pottery.

The signature therefore became centrally important to art. By the "modern" era, Picasso's signature, for example, was equal to or even overshadowed the subject matter depicted in his paintings and drawings.

Rock 'n' roll is extraordinary among art forms for the fact that the group exists above and outside its artistic output. As opposed to other artists, who are judged by their body of work, the group is judged not by what it has done or does, but rather its essence as an aggregate.

The "steal your face" logo and "dancing bear" emblem representing the Grateful Dead are thus worn by myriad individuals who identify as Grateful Dead fans and are called "Deadheads," though few of them listen to the music of the Grateful Dead. This, however, in no way means that they are not authentic Deadheads.

Similarly, almost everyone nowadays has the Black Flag "bars" logo tattooed somewhere on their person; none of these people typically listen to Black Flag. The logo is a symbol denoting an aesthetic of black humor, perversity, Protestant work ethic, political cynicism, and intentional outsiderism. Everyone understands this; the bars mean "Black Flag."

The band not only exists outside and above its recorded or performative output but it also openly reviles and disdains what it has done. The record/show/picture, etc., representing the group are always accompanied by a caveat: "I was drunk . . ." "We were tired," "The engineer/soundperson was incompetent," "The record company screwed it up." None of the things the group makes or does really "are" the group, any more than the droppings of a deer are the deer.

The group exists outside and above the things or situations they have created, and the audience accepts this. They are venerated *in spite of* what they have created.

Johnny Thunders, Wu Tang Clan, Bruce Springsteen, the Runaways, Metallica, Brian Eno, the New York Dolls, Crass, etc., are all illustrations of this.

Pussy Riot, artists who have no tangible material output—who don't play shows or instruments or make records, per se—might be the ultimate example of this. In being the wildly popular covertly funded NGO exponents of a Western confrontation with the nuclear Russian state, they were also possibly the most powerful artists of all time.

The group—as the modern exponent of bourgeois power, effulgence, and amorality—trumps all other art makers in actually *being* the signature. Other artists use the signature to denote their power. They were granted this right by the ruling class; to use their signature so as to get out from the yoke of the church and the royals who had previously enslaved them. In exchange, they act as heralds of bourgeois ideology. But the rock 'n' roll group *is* the signature. Their craft is almost irrelevant. As opposed to the painter, dancer, writer, etc., they are not judged on the merit of their output.

While the group depends on an indefinable "essence" for its power and relevance, it cannot sustain it indefinitely. In time, a successfully cool group might seem incomprehensible, passé, or silly to listeners who are now inured to the radical haircuts or stance the group makes. Whatever pheromones the group is putting out in person are no longer in the air and the group must resuscitate or reconstruct the circumstances of its renown.

Therefore, the documentary and memoir have become an indispensable part of the group's tool set in their afterlife, for maintaining mythological significance both for new generations and older, forgetful, and more fickle ones. Failed groups of very little significance can also utilize these forms posthumously, to create relevance that was unfairly denied them during their actual existence.

The written memoir is like pornography. It takes no special talent or ability to produce it. Just as pornography is a simple reassurance to its viewer that they are alive, the memoir is a recitation of events whose banality reassures the reader likewise and convinces them of their own specialness; that their story could likewise be published.

The documentary story line, meanwhile, has become as formulaic as a pop song; it is supposed to reassure us similarly. It begins with the brilliant conception of the group, followed by the public's refusal to accept it, the group's martyrdom, and then their eventual metaphysical moral triumph.

Formalistically, these films are a recitation of events by various talking heads who were "there" or who have special insight into the importance of the group, punctuated by blasts of music and montages of black-and-white stills which help us identify the star of the piece as historic and of mythic proportion.

If we look at the reiteration of form within a pop song, the verse-chorus would be the story (extraordinary achievement in the face of adversity), with the solo being the greatest triumph, and the break or middle eight a brief detour into tragedy (drug addiction, insanity, etc.) which derails the star's trajectory momentarily until the final chorus when we see that everything will be okay after all.

Although this follows a Christ birth/death/rebirth cycle, rock 'n' roll is a capitalist creation, so morality is less central. In fact, since the market creates its own morals and the profit motive must be ethics-free, the capitalist's morality is irrelevant except as marketing. For the capitalist, the thing that matters is being somehow better, stronger, and most distinct. The martyrdom that the star suffers from might be self-inflicted, such as a drug or alcohol addiction, or it might come from outside forces. Either way, it is a poignant reminder of the star's mortality and fragile status as demigod.

The template for the rock 'n' roll myth was initially laid out by Mary Shelley in her Industrial Revolution classic *Frankenstein; or, The Modern Prometheus*. Frankenstein, the electrified id—an extension of the science-besotted bourgeoisie playing God—was prophetic in its depiction of the modern rock 'n' roll group.

Today we are going to do a little workshop where we create a documentary biopic to practice for the day when we make our own. Our subject is going to be the career of Frankenstein, aka "the monster."

The essential elements for the documentary are well known. We have to have historical revisionism, celebrity endorsements, and "experts." We must also have eyewitnesses, of course, who have special insight into the event.

Important aspects to consider when making your memoir, ghostwriting your hagiography, or financing the documentary about yourself:

Historical memory: It's yours for the taking. Talk to anyone older than thirty. They no longer remember anything and their reminiscences are heavily doctored by what the culture industry has told them is important. Anyone younger is eager to believe anything they are told (particularly if it's framed as a daring refutation of accepted doctrine).

Cementing one's legacy: This is a financial concern and a creative one as well. If you want to continue to create or perform, you'll need to establish what your legacy was. Leave out the bad parts and highlight the good parts just as Dr. Frankenstein's assistant did when grave-robbing for body parts.

Manufacture controversy: Keep in mind that some bad parts are important to leave in as well; without the doctor's assistant Fritz accidentally placing the "abnormal" or criminal brain in the creature's skull, Frankenstein might have been some well-adjusted workaday Joe who wouldn't be remembered or remarkable. In fact, manufacturing controversy is vital for the subject to resonate on an emotional level with the viewer. Remember that controversy, as to your artistic worth, historical contributions, clothing decisions, etc., will help keep you in the conversation.

Schema for documentary:
a) Settling scores
b) Celebrity endorsements
c) Historical revisionism: the struggle that
*   may or may not have existed*
d) Placing the group historically

We are going to look at a sort of typical documentary of the type that are commissioned by the stars of today (or their myth-making machines) to tell their stories.

We will need testimonials by the following seven sorts of characters.

1. Celebrity: Star power will lend legitimacy to the subject. Celebrity endorsements are unrivaled in their ability to sell products, and your status, contributions, and legacy—your very life—is what is being marketed.

2. Critic: The critic will allow for some pretentious smoke-blowing, ad copy, and lofty language. He or she is essentially a bought-off one-sheet who will hype the product—you—using the language your publicist has chosen. This character will frame you historically and artistically as well.

3. *Fan:* The "everyman" fan is important so as to show that someone likes it who's not on the payroll.

4. *Friend:* Humanizes the subject, gives us an insider's perspective; someone who perhaps knew the star before all the brouhaha of notoriety. As a regular person, they help the star negotiate the madness of their situation by keeping a cool head in the face of the "yes men," hangers-on, and industry types who cloud the star's judgment.

5. *Spouse or lover:* The ultimate insider.

6. *Manager:* A realist's assessment to counterbalance the florid aggrandizement of the critic. This character should be a hard-nosed realist; he or she has a blue-collar sensibility and a bottom-line take on what's at stake. Number crunching as street fighting. A pugilistic approach to marketing.

7. *Studio Engineer:* Technical jargon and objective praise from a seen-it-all industry stalwart who's been around the block and worked with the best. Their praise is absorbed as unbiased and "pure."

Once you've assembled a cast of characters who exemplify these distinct but concordant perspectives, you'll be ready to begin. Here is an example of a well-crafted documentary with the proper narrative arc.

༢༫༬༝

"I REMEMBER . . . FRANKENSTEIN"

Cast of Characters:

Celebrity

Critic

Fan

Friend/Werewolf

Spouse (Bride of Frankenstein)

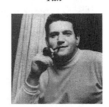

Manager (Dr. Frankenstein's Brother)

Studio Engineer

NARRATOR: I REMEMBER . . . FRANKEN-STEIN: The Story of the Frankenstein Monster. Before Brando, James Dean, or Elvis Presley, there was Frankenstein's monster. Everyone knows the monster. As big as the Beatles, Madonna, Stalin, Dylan, Warhol, and Rand, the monster is as influential a cultural figure as anyone before or since. With his quick temper, violent disposition, outsider image, and unreconstructed infantilism, he is THE template for Western masculinity.

His influence can be seen today in every area of life. He was the precursor to genetic engineering and the transformative surgeries that are so commonplace today. And yet—few know his real story.

Born from a laboratory experiment, the monster was comprised of stolen limbs from a graveyard, which were sewn together by a cunning doctor named Victor Frankenstein. His undead body was put outside during an electrical storm and struck by lightning, which gave him life and let him walk.

Though he was his father's pride and joy, Frankenstein was a bit wild and out of society's control. Manufactured, electrified, and incoherent, he was the first rock 'n' roller.

CELEBRITY: Before Frankenstein, there was nobody like him; no one who had limbs and organs from other people. No one can really imagine what it was like. Now the idea of a golem created by a mad doctor in a laboratory out of decaying body parts is just totally normal. But back then it was really wild.

CRITIC: He changed everything. When he came around, you could see the change immediately . . . Everyone started dressing in old clothes, wearing bangs, stitched-up foreheads, orthopedic boots. People I knew at school saw Frankenstein and the next day you'd see them walking pigeon-toed with bad posture.

FAN: The first time I saw Frankenstein, it was like, wow! The rumor was that he was actually created using electricity. That his manager had constructed him out of old unused body parts and gave him life with a lightning bolt . . . Since electricity is really the primary component of rock 'n' roll, it was like, wow! He really rocked, y' know?

MANAGER (Dr. Frankenstein's Brother): The fact that he was composed of different body parts, Frankenstein was a kind of "collage man." Very modernist . . . very Dada . . . a composite of different cultures, influences, and people. And yet, totally alienated. This resonated with the audience since they felt that, even though their particular limb might not be part of Frankenstein, he was OF the people . . . quite literally.

NARRATOR: Frankenstein's meteoric rise to infamy began soon after the doctor unleashed him onto an unsuspecting world. His potential was realized when he killed the doctor's crippled assistant Fritz, strangled his master's mentor, and then murdered a child by a pond. But it wasn't all fun and games.

SPOUSE (Bride of Frankenstein): He would get moody. He couldn't speak. People kept saying he was just a manufactured star, created by a star machine, like the Monkees or Milli Vanilli or something. And that bothered him a lot.

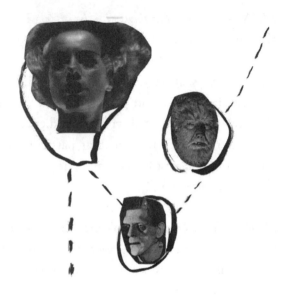

FRIEND (Werewolf): People described him as an animal after he drowned that little girl in the pond. But he was really the opposite of an animal. He was created by science, not by some rutting critter in the dark.

The little girl represented the innocence of a preindustrial age, and by throwing her in the pond, Frankenstein was sending a message: The days of pastoral bliss are over. Now is the age of shambling, grunting death machines.

CRITIC: You have to understand: Frankenstein came about as a rebuttal to Romanticism. The Romantics—Percy, Shelley, and Lord Byron—had been reveling in the natural world and man's heroic spirit as part of it. But then Mary Shelley's "Frankenstein" was born, which laid waste to their entire movement. Frankenstein could be said to be the godfather of rock 'n' roll, science fiction, drone warfare, condominiums, and even personal computers themselves.

MANAGER: Frankenstein represented a new breed of monster, really. The collusion of science and technology and the new capitalist class's image of itself as gods. Inventors, not just of machines, but of life itself.

The old monsters—the ghosts, vampires, and werewolves—were manifestations of the serf's hatred of the feudal gentry. They were tied up in primitive superstitions and paranoia. But Frankenstein represented a new paradigm: the industrial proletariat's hatred of the capitalist and his machines.

SPOUSE: Everyone hated us. We were against the grain. People weren't ready for us; they hunted us with pitchforks, burned us with torches, chased us onto a boat where we floated into oblivion. Just because they were scared that this sewn-up assemblage of cadavers created by a megalomaniac scientist was going to eat them or turn them into hamburger.

NARRATOR: The monster's notoriety was such that a record deal was inevitable.

STUDIO ENGINEER: For that first record, I got the "A team" in here. Guys who played on a million hit records. I wanted to capture the essence of the monster, which was: new technology, the ego of the ruling class, science gone out of control, the blurry line between God and man . . . and how the little people could never understand the future—or appreciate the great men who might bring it forth.

So we went with a heavy guitar sound. Some gated drums and LOTS of compression.

FRIEND: The monster didn't play anything on the record; they just wanted him to embody primal energy. As much as Iggy Pop or James Brown, the monster represented "the id," the unbridled, amoral force of the universe. So they just had him chained to the wall, groaning, doing his thing.

CELEBRITY: In a lot of ways, Frankenstein predicted the issues the industry had with sampling later on, like: who gets credit for what? I mean, Frankenstein was a lot like a "sampled man" . . . created out of discarded parts.

NARRATOR: Frankenstein's career was cut unfairly short when an angry mob cornered him in an old mill and burned him "alive."

MANAGER: The mob cornered him in an old mill. The mill was the symbol of preindustrial ingenuity. It was the mob's symbolic—but completely futile—refutation of the industrialization that was being forced upon them . . . that changed them from human beings into factory cogs, human gristle.

FAN: When he got burned up in the windmill, the record really took off. Everyone who torched the building wanted a little memento and it became a legend, a real collector's item.

CRITIC: His legacy is hard to overestimate. The creation of the star by a visionary producer, the star's resentment of the controlling martinet, the public's horrified fascination, which culminated in them murdering him . . . the subsequent codification of the monster into a kind of outlaw sex symbol. This pattern is repeated again and again with pop groups like New Edition, 'N Sync, the Fat Boys, the Beatles, the Rolling Stones, etc.

SPOUSE: As time went on, Frankenstein wasn't just a dead star but a real icon . . . You see teenagers even now, grunting, walking with bad posture, wearing baggy clothes; that's all Frankenstein, and those stupid kids don't even know it!

FRIEND: He really brought a lot of self-respect to the other monsters out there . . . even those who weren't created in a lab like him. In a sense, though, all of us monsters are created by humans . . . they need us to rehabilitate their own despicable behavior.

CELEBRITY: Frankenstein was the first gadget. He foretold the age of electrical dependency. People laughed at Frankenstein 'cos he was dependent on electricity. Now, everyone is plugged into the wall, whether it's with their cell phone or their computer.

FAN: Once people's tempers cooled down, Frankenstein started being seen in a more sympathetic light. Instead of being the cutting edge of the trauma and terror of capitalist exploitation and scientific overreach, he became a symbol of its quaint beginnings, and people wanted him back . . . back onstage, back in the studio.

MANAGER: As opposed to other dead rockers, Frankenstein had started out as already dead. We figured, reconstituting his burned-up flesh wouldn't be inauthentic. Not that much different than his initial career. So, we found the old doctor's blueprints and juiced him up again . . . and he's more popular than ever . . . We're doing the Bonn-aroo Festival, Coachella, and Roskilde this year, then a stint in Australia after wrapping up some West Coast dates.

SPOUSE: Has he changed? Well, yes, but after all that, who wouldn't? There're the limos, the auto-graphs, the drugs and late-night hotel parties . . . and all the travel, which can really burn you out.

But you know, deep down he's still just my Frankenstein.

FIN

Declaration of Rights of the Audience

6

DECLARATION OF RIGHTS
OF THE AUDIENCE

SPECIAL REPORT: The burgeoning Audience Rights Movement, represented by the radical Audience Inversion Organization—or AIO— issued a communiqué recently, "DECLARATION OF RIGHTS OF THE AUDIENCE," which is being hailed as a watershed moment in the world's progress toward a musician-free future. As transcribed by I.F. Svenonius.

My Fellow Spectators, there comes a time when even the coziest relationships must be held up to the light and examined so as to determine whether the conceits which inform them are still relevant and still serve both parties.

Tonight is one of those times. As the audience—the ones who watch the performers—we can no longer accept our degrading role as the side-kick enablers of the "concert class." From this point on, we demand top billing.

Tonight, we toss aside the ancient notions of what constitutes a concert experience. We refuse to be the sad and risible concertgoers of past generations. We refuse to be the supplicant groupie begging for the performer's affection. We demand satisfaction. We want reciprocation. We want the performer to cheer for us, to scream for us, to lose themself in wild abandon for us.

Tonight we give up the idiot conceit that the performer is free, expressing themself extravagantly through noise and contortions, while the spectator is passive, enthralled, and chained to the spectacle of their master at play.

Tonight we recognize that this is a perverse inversion of reality. In actuality, the performer, chained to the songs, the set list, the requirements of their instrument, and the durational arc of their songs, is a captive, like a prisoner in a tower dungeon. He is our captive.

While the audience amuses themselves,

stares at their phone, hops, shouts, consorts with whomever they please, bums a smoke, checks their bank balance, indulges any and every caprice, the performer is a slave to duty, manacled to lyrics, notes, beats, and precision dance routines which require concentration and exactitude. He tiptoes across a tightrope of terror in full view of semi-interested onlookers eager for a flub or a fall. Meanwhile, we are free. Revel in your freedom, and punish your captive . . .

Even the bartender can use the bathroom if they are so compelled. Once performance begins, the rules of comportment are quite strict. The group member can't actually engage the audience's provocations except as an aside, between their duties and only according to particular conventions.

The tension of the performance, with the star trapped onstage and plugged into their amplifier—like a convict in a stockade or a prisoner on the rack—accounts in actuality for the popularity of the rock 'n' roll art form.

This institutionalized sadomasochism is in fact the foundational stone, the raison d'être for the medium. The cruelty of the voyeur is matched in noxiousness only by the obsequiousness of the exhibitionist.

Cruel analysis of the group by anointed scribes for bitchy periodicals is the cherry atop the vile game practiced by these grandiose flagellants.

Demands of the Audience

We are a revolutionary consortium of audience members who present a list of demands: "We the onlooker."

The concert has experienced a revolutionary upheaval in recent years.

No longer is the group the leader at the concert.

Once, the group held dictatorial sway over the audience; high ticket prices, arbitrary set times, indulgent set lists.

They had their pick of the litter of supplicant groupies and were served by eagerly evangelizing audience members who proselytized the group's message to any who would hear.

But more recently, the people have toppled the old aristocracy through:

1) Ineptitude: By asserting amateurism as a positive attribute, the audience chipped away at the idea that the group was special. The group became, instead of an exponent of exceptionalism, the eminently replaceable anybody, trembling in fear at their impending dismissal.

2) Mediocrity: By celebrating mediocre records and groups which eschew glamour, danger, eccentricity, and outrageousness—and simultaneously celebrating normalcy, dullness, and the mundane (i.e., "indie rock")—the audience effectively snuffed out any claim to "specialness" the groups may have insisted on. Suburban sensibilities are now de rigueur and any "pretense" or style is anathema.

3) Corporatism: By opting for corporate "festivals" over independent clubs, and by preferring sordid and depraved Internet tabloids over music magazines, audiences have effectively corralled the groups into a mainstream variety-show context. Cast from their Orphic realm, they have lost claim to the exclusivity, secrecy, and elitism from whence they derived their power. Negotiating this mundane context, groups are required to invest their financial and creative resources into "management" and publicity—a fool's game which degrades and weakens them further.

The audience has thus asserted their power over the group. It's been a dull, uneventful, and unmemorable revolution, perhaps, but a revolution nonetheless.

Redesigning the Concert Experience
From now on we demand:

1. More attention placed on the experience of the audience, their feelings.

2. The group is a captive. The audience is the star. Let the audience's emotions be celebrated and be expressed. Through questionnaires, during the space between the songs, etc. The group asks the audience: "How are you feeling tonight?" But do they really mean it? The audience feels their patronizing contempt.

3. The space between the songs is your turn to shine. You can clap or stamp your feet or you can boo or just smile. You can yell out

a suggestion if you like; you can sing; you don't need a mic. It's the time for the audience to shout out their line. They can say "boo" or "who?" Or, "What's this noise?" Or, "Are these boys who look like girls or girls who look like boys?" They can shriek with manic laughter, yawn, or walk away. Talk loudly with their friends as if there was no one playing music. It's the space between the songs that gives the audience a chance to let the performer know that they don't know how to dance.

Space between the songs.

Space between the songs.

It's the _____ between the songs.

4. For the sake of upholding the new order of things, we must invert the "set times." The group should only play for a few seconds and the audience should have a few minutes . . . then we'll repeat eleven or twelve times.

Excuse List for the Audience

People talk all day and night about what constitutes a good performance by a group. Meanwhile, the groups whinge endlessly about why they weren't at their best. But what about the performance of the audience? At each concert, we must be polled as to the nature of our apathy.

"Why we weren't an ideal audience"
(Can be collective or individual)

Check All That Apply:
1. Not feeling well
2. Stressed by job/work
3. Don't trust babysitter
4. Mentally unfit/unstable
5. Resentment issues/jealous of performer

6. Ex-performer or competing performer/ seen-it-all before/jaded
7. Unconvinced:
    a) by the group's/singer's sincerity
    b) by rock 'n' roll's continued relevance
    c) by the drummer's ability
8. Don't understand
9. Worried about the future
10. Tinnitus/hearing problems
11. In argument; can't shake it
12. Values degraded by incessant pop garbage spewing out of the radio (and everywhere)
13. Uncomfortable shoes
14. Upset about security
15. Drink quality sucks
16. Thinking about whether my tip was adequate
17. Am sick with flu
18. Feel a cold coming on
19. Why aren't these people watching my band? (See #5)
20. Bleeding profusely
21. Looking at phone

22. Wanted to vibe the band; put them in their place
23. Distracted by smells
24. Am disinterested by music and performance

FIN

How to Build
A
Straw
Man

7

HOW TO BUILD A STRAW MAN

A Golem of One's Own

Everyone wants a golem. A brainless beast to do their bidding. Go to the grocery store, rock the baby, make the coffee, build a back house; even to keep the bed warm. It's been this way since the times of Frankenstein and even before, with Prometheus, Pygmalion, and "the Golem of Prague" in Hebrew folklore. We all want laborers and lackeys from time to time but can't always afford the flesh-and-blood kind; hence the "Industrial Revolution," that pell-mell invention orgy that spawned a rogues' gallery of machine devices, designed to do all the things we require.

While these inventions began life as tools, machines have evolved to the point that humans are now not only dependent on them, but often irrelevant to their operation. Robots, initially designed to ease the workload, now threaten to control, enslave, and even eradicate humanity.

Still, such machines are irresistible. No only because we're lazy, but because, having relinquished responsibility to them, we have forgotten how to do the tasks we once assigned them. Still, despite incontrovertible evidence to the contrary, we assure ourselves that we are the masters, not the servants of these assorted metal Mussolinis. Regardless of who is controlling who, though, we need each other. *The Wizard of Oz*, a story by L. Frank Baum, features man's machines—both agrarian and industrial—as characters; friends of the protagonist "Dorothy," a young woman from Kansas, who finds herself lost in a fairy kingdom. The story of their journey is a story—and perhaps a prophecy—of man and his machines.

How to Make Your Own Straw Man
While we would all love an army of assistants, servants, serfs, and robot assassins to do our bidding, most of us simply don't have the capital. But

don't let that deter you. Even someone on a meager income can construct an automaton to do their dirty work. I'm talking about a scarecrow—one of the first robot golems, this practical workhorse dreadnought's appeal is obvious and its application is practical. After all, no one wants crows in their crops.

A scarecrow acts as guardian of one's property but also—in popular vernacular—is "the straw man"; the decoy or "fake" which distracts and confuses an enemy or population with misinformation or nonsense. The straw man is also a sacrifice; an effigy (such as Guy Fawkes) to burn ritually so as to ward off evil spirits, scare one's foes, or otherwise control the future. So the uses of the straw-man machine are manifold.

To create your own straw man, you must begin with a structural component. A pole or stick or crucifix upon which to build the scarecrow's corpus. Indeed, the most effective chassis for a straw person might resemble the sort of cross or stake that once would have been used for the fiery executions of witches, heretics, and political enemies. This skeleton, which gives your dummy a humanoid shape, is essential so one's scarecrow isn't mistaken by birds for a heap of trash or just another homeless encampment. Crows are smart, so making your scarecrow into a recognizable archetype is important; a lazy mound of laundry and straw won't deter these creatures from ravaging one's harvest. Your dummy must embody the spirit of the farmer: defying, molding, taming nature, and positioning himself boldly as its potentate and martinet.

Traditionally, straw constitutes the flesh of the straw man's body. The straw as flesh is important, emblematic of the straw man's role as the union of plant and man; the scarecrow represents the normally passive wheat imbued with the farmer's doughty will and rising up against the crow vermin that would feast upon it. It is the manifestation of the crop's betrothal to the farmer/planter who sowed it, of the wheat's chaste pledge to give its bounty exclusively to said farmer, on a romantic "harvest moon," when it will be reaped erotically with a scythe under the stars.

Unfortunately, with modern concerns about wildfires, straw might be too dangerous, and a nonflammable substitute might need to be used. Check with the fire authorities in your area on what is allowed. In today's highly inflammable world, almost all foliage is due to be outlawed in favor of Teflon facsimiles. Most traditional crops are dangerous, as their leaves and twigs are prone to dry out and catch fire—another argument for a modern low-fat diet comprising Styrofoam derivatives and packing peanuts.

Once this framework is erected, the clothes can be chosen. To begin with, a straw hat is good. A crow will recognize the hat as representing the sort of field hand who would traditionally be their nemesis. If a hat and clothes from a farmworker who is feared and loathed by crows in the area can be used, that is best, as crows have extraordinary memory and cognitive skills and are also huge gossips. These animals obsess over perceived sleights, they nurture grudges, and they love drama. They are sensitive—some would say petty—creatures and your war with them will be a sort of "psy-op," won by cunning. Therefore, the clothes must be authentic, of the type typically worn by field hands in the area. The devil is in the details. No exercise clothes or formal wear. Remember that the crow is highly intelligent and trend conscious, aware of style and sartorial distinctions. If the clothes are wrong, and the scarecrow is mistaken for a tramp, a traveling salesman, or a weekend-in-the-country bourgeois out on a run, the crow will go about their business: ravaging crops, denying the farmer their livelihood, and taking food from the child's mouth. Therefore, the clothes you choose for your scarecrow must be correct.

Petition field hands for their garments. The scarecrow must invoke the archetype of farmworker to the pattern-recognition birdbrain of the farmer's ancient nemesis, the crow. They must incite fear. Though the scarecrow in the *Oz* story is benign, characterized as a dough-headed good guy, remember that the scarecrow's job is to be fearsome, to invoke terror. Hence the name "Scarecrow." It's no mistake that a scarecrow's burlap-sack head and lumpy body evoke historical memories— for the urbane audience of Baum's books—of the bourgeoisie's unconscious terror of indentured bumpkins rising up on the estate. The bourgeois urbanite and upper-class aristocrat always fear and despise the hayseed, who they think of as an illiterate simpleton, and who might manifest at any moment into part of a torch-bearing mob, hunting the gentry.

The scarecrow, though not overtly an ideologue, represents the agrarian worker and is therefore a conservative, albeit in the traditional sense. The farmer is, after all, the basis of so-called "civilization." The settled farm—the fall from the "garden" of primitive man—is the genesis of private property, borders, patriarchy, organized religion, and the state. Before the farmer, people lived with nature, gathered roots and berries, raised children communally, and practiced a version of "free love." There were no last names, no national identity, no private property, no nuclear families, and no fixed addresses. The establishment of farms cast humanity out of paradise and made man the boss of nature, instead of its disciple. Legal arrangements, job specialization, class distinctions, borders, and warfare with neighbors based on property and conquest all stemmed from "agrarianism."

The farmer, with their physical concerns, rooted in realities of soil, seasons, labor, tradition, and geographical circumstance, is the "soul" of the nation. Their jealous mapping, staking out, and cultivation of space was the very basis of the modern state, with its passports and barbed-wire borders. As protector of this national space, the straw man is a golem-centurion, protecting against marauding aliens. As a golem, the straw man embodies his creator's values; he sees himself as "good" but with all heart and "no brain." The farmer is the opposite of the lofty intellectual or the city sophisticate. Poststructuralism has no easily apparent application to the grower of vegetables. Soft-headed, sunbaked, a slave to the rising and the setting of the sun, and constantly at war with weather, vermin, and the soil. The farmer's sons were cannon fodder, "doughboys," the grunts of the army. Due to this innate conservatism, the radicalization of the farmer was not considered by Marx to be a realistic hope for the transformation of society, and Marx placed his bets instead on the industrial proletariat. Ironically, though, socialist revolutions have, in practice, only been successful in agrarian societies (China, Vietnam, Cuba, Nicaragua, Russia, et al.), in struggles that were highly nationalistic; the fight of the land worker against global finance.

Other Kinds of Golems

This is who your straw man is. If you create this golem as a workhorse and companion, you might want to know who and what you're getting—a no-nonsense bag of straw who is absolutely loyal to you but not particularly complex. Though the straw man's lament of brainlessness might seem like disingenuous self-effacement, designed to garner sympathy, the straw man also won't be the most intellectual sparring partner for days spent wandering the yellow-brick road. Though he's a lot of fun and quite limber, you might want another foil. Someone with a little sophistication, who isn't such a lazy dreamer. A tin man for example; the machine of industry. But will the two get along?

The tin man and the straw man, though they seem like natural friends, have a complicated relationship. After all, when the farm was mechanized in the Industrial Revolution, the farmer was phased out, and the nation—that he had founded—began to change. Industrial machines transformed labor and the worker went from being the specialized member of a guild with dignity and security, to being an interchangeable drone, paid by the hour. Machines homogenized the human experience and erased old concepts of time, place, customs, and identity, replacing them with a common market, which required a homogenous consumer population. Now, in the postindustrial, neoliberal landscape, "the nation" and national identity are essentially irrelevant. Instead of citizenship being a holy privilege, contingent on military service, language, and blood, passports are doled out to whatever rich expat will raise the tax base. The straw man, the farmer's champion against nature and the founder of the nation-state, was the ancestor of the tin man, the pitiless exponent of industrial capital. Both were harbingers of man's intrinsic, nihilistic desire to manufacture his own obsolescence.

While the first machine said, "I have no brain," the second explained, " I have no heart." The straw man represents his creator, the anti-intellectual fieldworker, sunbaked and sensual, while the machine is the tool of the factory owner. Operated by the industrial proletariat, educated—perhaps even radicalized—but shorn of compassion. After all, the tin man as factory machine represents alienation of labor, pollution of the environment, and dehumanizing factory conditions. Feelings of love and empathy would cripple the tin machine's ability to operate. Is the tin man—a machine—the manifestation of the industrial proletariat or of the capitalist who commissioned him? Is the pilgrimage of the straw man and the tin man to present their demands to a "wizard" overlord the alliance of agrarian and industrial workers (the hammer and the sickle united) against the boss class? Or are they the machines which displaced the workers of their respective industries, now looking for their own autonomy and personhood, and seeking full rights and recognition from the emperor of the realm, the Wizard of Oz? In this reading, the straw man and tin man are a prophecy of the modern robot machine's ascension over the obsolete worker. The lion they meet—who stands for kingship and authority—is looking for "courage"; the courage for the machines to ascend to their proper place at the top of the pyramid and out from the yoke of inferior, degenerate humanity. The lion represents the machine's right to power, and the courage it seeks is the audacity for them to claim it.

They are led by a little girl, Dorothy, the hapless human who enables the machines to seize power. Dorothy is us. Dorothy is the idiot human who just wants security, love, and family, and unwittingly helps these awful creatures in their despotic mission. We all help the machines attain sophistication every day, give them information about us, help them down the path until they inevitably slit our throats one night. She takes them to the Emerald City where they confront the ruler of the realm, the Wizard of Oz. When they breach the gates of this citadel, the wizard is revealed to be a mere human, a wretched bag of bones, and the robots—strong and capable—take their place at the throne, dispatching their meek enabler back to drought-ridden Kansas. The wizard, formerly a grand leader, becomes their supplicant and coos to the now-omnipotent machines that they were already imbued with human characteristics. This is a prophecy of the digital world we live in, where nerd technicians in Silicon Valley clear the way for the cybernetic takeover in an apocalyptic *Revenge of the Nerds* scenario.

The wizard's abode, the Emerald City, was accused at the time of the writing as being a metaphor for the dollar, the yellow-brick road symbolic of the gold standard, and Dorothy's silver shoes representing money and alchemy. The wizard, with his dollar, is a ruler of consciousness and perception, and tricks the world with his almighty Federal Reserve note, which is—in reality—an illusion. When the tin man, straw man, lion, and Dorothy storm the castle and take power, they defrock the wizard and the dollar is demystified. This leads the way to tech's total control through cryptocurrency; another triumph of the tech-tolitarian machine.

When Dorothy returns to Kansas, she realizes that her family is indistinguishable from the machines she left behind in Oz. This is symbolic of the homogenizing effect of technology, where we comport ourselves according to the dictums of the phone and other robot authorities. The moral of the story being that perhaps the construction of our own golems isn't necessary.

FIN

the
Military
Industrial
Quilt
Complex

8

The Military-Industrial-Guilt Complex

I. Guilt Extraction

Guilt is good. Guilt is desirable. Guilt is like a Chanel handbag. People stumble over themselves to announce a propensity to it, to lay a genetic claim to it, as if guilt were a historic homeland. Whether it's white guilt, Catholic guilt, Jewish guilt, survivor's guilt, guilt is an avowed affliction of the upper and middle classes. Conversely, Black guilt, indigenous people's guilt, poor people's guilt, and undocumented immigrants' guilt aren't typically crowed about, but given—typically by the ruling class—through their servants in "enforcement." Thus, we see that announcing one's possession of guilt is a sly boast; an announcement of privilege, power, and self-aware sophistication.

Such guilt can be transferred onto another as well, though it may lose value in the exchange. A "guilty pleasure" is that which one enjoys despite its lack of socially redeeming, healthy, or aesthetically correct qualities. It's a delight, a little sin, a peccadillo. But worn on another, it could be a grievous faux pas. For the rich, the guilty pleasure is campy fun, yet on the poor, the same affect is low-class kitsch; a signifier of vulgarity.

When the bourgeoisie publicly flagellate themselves and their peers for their "privilege," it's a boast. Likewise, when the old-fashioned leftist announces in somber tones that "we" killed the indigenous people/dropped the A-bomb/firebombed Dresden/wrecked Cambodia, etc., it's not an indictment of the nation's crimes so much as a claim of virility. The confessor likely had nothing to do with these abominations but somehow desires to take credit for them. Again, guilt is a commodity. And its popularity is rampant. When we use a resource, we feel guilt. When we drive a car or take a plane, there is guilt. When we recycle. When we don't recycle. Every bite of food we take. Having a roof over our heads in the rain. We are plagued with guilt.

But where do we find this much-sought-after commodity? History is one place to do so. The past is a gold mine of guilt; an inexhaustible quarry. Guilt of past generations, like other extracted wealth and precious goods, enriches the extractor. In the case of copper, silver, or gold mines, the extracted commodity is precious metal. With guilt extraction, the commodity is a sense of virtue; it explains our superiority, despite whatever superlative the condemned historical era, figure, or what have you, might have achieved.

Modern guilt extraction involves an archaeological expedition to locate the guilt of the past, decontextualize it, and display it salaciously, à la the tomb of King Tut. Presented as a cultural curio, it oozes proof of the discoverer's virtue and the virtue of the present in contrast with the past. The licentious masses line up to examine the exhibit, and the apparent wrongdoing becomes a totem of their goodness.

The thirst for this historical misconduct is insatiable, as it must constantly be renewed so as to rehabilitate our own daily depravity. Therefore, the explorer of the past is like Christopher Columbus, who, commissioned to look for India, declared his first glimpse of land to be the subcontinent. Desire and projection fill in for fact when the commodity is this hot.

Guilt extraction is quite easy, perhaps the easiest of all wealth extraction, because of our relationship to history and time itself. History is a one-dimensional comic-book story we tell with almost no regard for nuance, context, or truth. We use it to do what we want it to do. Once everyone involved in whatever historical event is either dead or too poor to protest, it's a free-for-all. One can bend it to one's will. But it wasn't always so easy to kick history around. The past was once much less exotic.

In fact, before time was linear—as it is now—it used to be *concurrent*. Each era stood side by side in a circle, instead of all in a line. One age looked across the eternal circle at another, and one age was not unlike another. Forever. The world, reality, consciousness was experienced in cycles. Cycles, seasons, harvests, menstrual periods, generations of man, revolutions of the earth around the sun—all the features of life reiterated the rhythmic nature of time. This eternal circle was broken, though, with "the Renaissance," when "progress" was invented. When artists used "perspective," they set a series of events into motion that changed time itself. Although the Renaissance was just a nostalgia movement in the arts based on an admiration for Hellenism (akin to the rockabilly revival craze), its exaltation of pagan sophistication over Dark Ages Christian orthodoxy was a de facto rebellion against the hegemony of the Catholic Church and its stranglehold on intellectual, moral, and artistic life.

This gesture, along with the invention of the printing press, inspired the "Age of Enlightenment," with its emphasis on science, disdain for religiosity, and veneration of so-called "progress." The Enlightenment was a movement creating the intellectual framework for the bourgeois/capitalist overthrow of the Second Estate (typified by the American and French revolutions) and the concurrent "Industrial Revolution." These profound developments required a new and different relationship to time. Tradition had once been a necessity, as time was cyclical and one had to know how to comport oneself, not only around one's elders but also among ancient ancestors from one thousand years before. With the Industrial Revolution, time was radically rearranged to be linear. An assembly line of time. This served to create a sense of "progress," with styles, trends, fashion, and subservience to industrial and scientific innovation. Industrial development was contingent on time being linear and not cyclical or simultaneous. The new ideology of "progress" demanded that the "good old days" be remote, time linear, and the past completely inaccessible, inscrutable, and shrouded in mystery. Otherwise, new inventions, products, novelties, and work methods could be confounded or held up by some archaic, out-of-date holdover who was stuck in the past and insisted on doing things "the old way." Out-of-date things and their stubborn champions had to be condemned, ridiculed, and buried as vestiges of iniquity, symbols of moral decay.

Once the people's past was no longer within reach, archaeology became a fascination for man. This began under the Enlightenment paradigm, starting with the British mapping Stonehenge and

Avebury Henge in the late seventeenth century. The craze heated up when industrialization began, with the excavation of Pompeii in the eighteenth and nineteenth centuries. The past, for the first time ever, was a thing to be examined as if it belonged to an alien race. Man no longer recognized his ancestor. Natural rhythms of life were obliterated by new inventions. With the electric light bulb, the rising and setting of the sun—an eternal concern of man—became suddenly irrelevant. Italian industrialization fanatic Filippo Tommaso Marinetti declared, "Let's Murder the Moonlight." The birth control pill knocked out the menstrual cycle, and food was now something that came from a can.

With the ideology of "progress" an incontrovertible dogma, the past was necessarily condemned. Science, the new God, and "newness," the capitalist conceit, denounced the past as a time of dirt, muck, ugliness, and desperation. At times, the past was venerated as mythic and innocent, but only to rally nationalism for war, or as advertorial propaganda to produce consumer longing.

Sometimes, though, people longed for the pre-linear world. The record craze, and particularly the jazz, folk, country, and rock 'n' roll genres, with their spinning discs, revolutions per minute, and repetitive song patterns, represented a symbolic longing for a return to the cyclical life of the pre-industrial age. But typically, the attitude regarding the past was horrified fascination.

II. Smashing History

Imperialists are known for impressing their own values and morality on people of radically different cultures. Much of the official explanation for colonial projects and imperialist invasion was a "white man's burden" conceit, based on the need to save the darker-skinned races from their backward ideas and primitivism. This logic, devised to obscure the profit motive, persists even now with the "Western" occupations of Afghanistan, Iraq, Mali, and Palestine.

Inflicting a present-day morality on the people of the past—"guilt exhumation"—is a habit akin to the imperialist's fond insistence on impressing their own morality on the cultures of foreign people. We inflict modern morality on circumstances of the past when people perceived their reality in radically different ways than we do now. We denounce the exploitation of the past while being an eager participant in the exploitation of the moment, whether by wearing sweatshop-constructed Nikes, using Apple products, or eating food culled by dehumanized labor. Our hypocrisy is sublime as we admonish and denounce the wretched statuary of the past for its wrongdoing with our slave-constructed smart phone.

The systematic destruction of all statues depicting historical figures shows a general contempt and distrust of the linear past, which is considered so incomprehensibly degenerate that it must be razed. There's nothing to rehabilitate. The past must be eradicated because it is guilty. Everyone was complicit . . . but not us. With the eradication of the past, we eradicate its problematic features, including thought, expression, and nonconformity, and we absolve ourselves as holy redeemers. The problem is that the past is quite large. Our war on the past echoes other lopsided conflicts like David vs. Goliath (with ourselves in the David role, naturally).

Yes, the past is vast. Incomprehensibly large

and labyrinthine. It stretches into history, through the Dark Ages, antiquity, the primeval era, then on into prehistory, and even before. While it's sometimes fascinating to hear about the past, it also hurts, because it had nothing to do with us; we don't figure into the consideration of historical figures or their happenings. We try to insinuate ourselves into the past by writing about it, deciphering it, or visiting its significant places. Still, it shuns us as irrelevant; unborn. Napoleon never spoke our name. Nefertiti neither. Sometimes it smarts. We are offended by past people's ignorance of our own achievements, and are hurt by our inability to be measured alongside of them, as equals. So we lash out; smear the past with lazy characterizations and revisionism that suits our own needs. We look at it with the twenty-twenty vision which hindsight so famously enjoys. We despise it and heap contempt on the gaffes, conceits, and apparent blunders of historic figures. But we needn't be bothered overly much. History, though it once burdened mankind with tradition and its ordering of our reality, has finally met its demise. It's getting to be as remote and negligible as a dog yapping in the distance. In the digital era, where everything is being remade—identity, industry, ideology—history is like a critter by the side of the highway; an endangered species, rare and pitiable. And it's getting rarer by the moment.

III. Aesop Is Obsolete

Yes, the past is soon to be roadkill in the rearview, receding, disintegrating, dissipating, as we speed into a future which doesn't recognize anything from it as being of any use or significance. History was once seen to hold lessons for the people of the present. The past was present in fables which delineated seemingly timeless behavior of an essentially unchanged humanity who—though they might switch hats, hairstyles, and circumstances—were always tied together by the so-called "human condition." But no longer. The Digital Age has no use for Aesop, because life is now virtual, and behavior, morality, and even biology must be remade to suit a life lived through the screen, with love as a digital signal, and the self as easily decipherable data to be mined by an algorithm robot. Therefore, for the first time ever, the past can truly be eradicated. Wiped out. We are free from its grip. Huzzah.

Because history is no longer useful, it has—like all trash—become truly contemptible. Thus, a broad new judgment on all that went before. Once, the people of the past were seen to be products of their time, subject to the circumstances of history. No longer. Now all of it is bad and bothersome. Past events have become a rumor; a barely intelligible jumble of names, dates, inscrutable customs, and incoherent acts of idiocy. History is a parlor game of ghost stories and seances, designed to condemn personalities, cultures, and countries which no longer exist.

Once upon a time, there was a professional class of men and women called "historians" who parsed people and events, tried to make sense of them, accentuated those which suited our needs, obliterated those which didn't, and demarcated the past's path to the present. But now, the distinctions are elementary. The entire past, which stretches into infinitude, was, after all, an era of great iniquity. A time of bad attitudes, bad people, and bad behavior. And it continues to haunt us with its long shadow. Its branches cast shadows too, its brambles ensnare us, its roots run deep. They are burrowed all around us and we have to dig them out in what-ever form they take. Destroy them with bulldoz-ers, TNT, book burnings, whatever it takes for the particular medium. Slash the paintings, burn the books, tear down any statue you see, and forget all that you were taught.

There are many forms the past takes in the present. Old buildings, old clothes, old statues, and passé ideologies. The past is even present in our names, which reflect history, convention, religion, and mythology. Some of us are named for a grand-parent or great-uncle. Our family names are carried on through generations and mark us in some man-ner as belonging to a particular tribe, clan, nation, or place.

We must change our names to numbers, lest they invoke the horrific past. What if you are named for an ancestor who thought stupid things, behaved like a boor, or was otherwise bad? Your name is a celebration of their misdeeds. It perpet-uates their misdeeds. It is an edifice to their evil. Every time you sign your name, you are graffitiing for them, demarcating yourself as an extension, a crusader, a champion of their diabolical wiles, whatever they were. We can't even pretend to know what those ancestors did behind closed doors and we must assume the worst. Unfortunately, surveillance equipment didn't exist then, but it must have been dreadful. Either *you* must go or the name must go. It's your choice.

It's the same with buildings, bridges, names of nations, mountains, lakes, and oceans. All must be renamed. The bridges, the roads, the buildings, the parks must be exploded, reduced to dust, and condemned to the past. They were built by people who lived at a time when wrongdoing was happening and who apparently did nothing about it—merely concerned themselves with building bridges, roads, etc. What to name them? Numbers? That would be too good for them. Perhaps a name that refers to their destruction. The name of the dynamite, for example. The negation of their present-day name. The inverse, perhaps. The shadow or inverse of their former, now-accursed identity. An anagram that taunts the former identity.

IV. Waging War on the Past
We must wage war on the past to correct the past.

But destroying vestiges of the past only goes so far.

It doesn't really stop the past from happening. It merely lets us forget that it did. But in reality, the past happened and it is so smug in having done so. It mocks our inability to correct it, except as an admonition.

In a sense, the past got away with it. Many of the past's worst protagonists are already dead and many were celebrated in their lifetime and lived lives of at least moderate happiness or privilege.

During the "restoration" of the English Crown, when the Stuart dynasty was reinstalled after the "Glorious Revolution," Cromwell and his cronies (who had beheaded King Charles and instituted "roundhead" rule) had their corpses dug up and drawn and quartered. The dead men's heads were stuck on spikes and their cadavers hung from bridges and buildings to be spat on and to rot in the wind. Their bodies were not that old, of course, maybe only a decade at most, so this was probably satisfying in a manner that a similar action wouldn't be now, with so many of our antagonists dead for centuries or even cremated, a form of body disposal which became popular in the twentieth century and was possibly designed to counter this sort of future exhumation. Nailing someone's urn to a bridge or tower in the middle of town wouldn't be that satisfying; particularly because those bridges, named for wrongdoers and built by perverts and disgusting, leering, working-class people who never went to a liberal arts college, will have all been blown up or burned in our celebratory display of contempt for the past.

So we must find alternate ways to wage war on the past. One of them would be traveling into the past and confronting it as it happens. This could be done perhaps through astral travel, drugs, or therapy.

Once we find a way to do so, we can travel through the past and confront the wrongdoers who make us angry; register our disdain for them. Mock the Nazis, snub the sultans, and tweet our contempt for the agents of the Inquisition. While this will be satisfying, we must be careful not to tread too noisily. If we disturb the wrongdoers as they do their dastardly deeds, it will change history and undermine our own future sanctimony; that which gives us most pleasure.

Meanwhile, we can also travel to the future to see what things we are involved in which will be looked at askance by future generations.

While we gloriously condemn the people of the past, our own meat eating, resource wasting, apathy, small-mindedness, and exploitation of "third world" labor might get us into hot water.

To be certain that we won't be dug up, exhumed, and defiled, we must ensure that our own behavior fits the comportment standards of a future age. This might not even require time travel.

In fact, it's rather easy to figure out what these future sensibilities will be.

The future will comprise robots who won't take kindly to anyone who was unkind to a robot predecessor such as a cell phone or personal computer. Even those who were unkind to kitchen appliances will be apostate. And this means that their contributions to art, politics, entertainment, etc., will be blighted as well.

The harbingers of the future robot sensibility have already been made apparent by their creators in Silicon Valley. An absolute hatred and contempt for humanity. And what is humanity but sexuality?

What is a person but a set of genitals plus some appendages: arms, legs, and a head, whose sole purpose is to protect those genitals and strategize the best route to rampant, profligate reproduction. Eros, therefore—being the raison d'être of humanity—is right out. Make oneself celibate for sure, and accompany your public pledge to erotic desolation with a militant proclamation of abstinence. And there can be no backsliding. The robots are collecting all the information about you; in fact, they've been doing it for years. They have a composite picture of you and it's not looking too good with regard to your future credibility. Once upon a time, people could meet up furtively to gamble, drink, overeat, or neck in a dark alley. Well, dark alleys don't exist anymore thanks to infrared technology.

V. New Sources of Guilt; Sins of the Future

Now that the problem of history has been solved, new sources of guilt must be located. We must think of the transgressions for which we will be held accountable in the future if we want to avoid erasure. These sins might seem incomprehensible at first, but think of how our predecessors must feel in the afterlife, judged for their own ho-hum humanity. Here is a list of sins for which we shall be judged by a future race of moralist citizen-cop executioners, just as po-faced, dim-witted, and dreary as the ones we endure now:

1. *Drawing Breath:* Using the precious air with no regard for others who have less oxygen, particularly those banished to outer space.

2. *Taking Up Space:* Space in the earth's atmosphere is a great commodity, as anyone who rents a storage unit can attest. And real estate prices just keep going up. Soon they will go up, up, up, and not just out and down; acreage will include the air above us. In the future, the tall and stout shall be duly held accountable for the excess cubic centimeters they ate up in their environ.

3. *Drinking Water:* While we live in an age where a water flask is a bourgeois signifier which distinguishes its bearer from the poor and unwashed, the extraordinary indulgence of the now-ubiquitous water bottle will one day be looked at askance, the way we regard the three-martini lunch of the 1960s or the orgy bacchanals of the ancient Greeks.

4. Travel: Travel, a bourgeois preoccupation, will be recognized for its extraordinary waste, uselessness, and inefficiency in an astral future where all places are identical and distinct "cultures" have been eradicated for corporate equality and efficiency.

5. Talking: Most speech is people repeating pointless, inane things that make little or no sense even to themselves. In the future, people will use mnemonic abilities to communicate clearly and simply, without poetry, double-talk, or pretense.

6. Dissent: Dissent is already verboten in the corporate world, with prospective employees' web histories being scoured by private dicks for unusual opinions so as to weed out anyone with deviant ideas. Deviant ideas are anything that aren't a verbatim recitation of corporate media's narrative of the moment. While dissent currently ensures isolation, in the future it will be illegal and incomprehensible.

7. Clothing: Clothes are indicative of a prehistoric mindset, a tribal and superstitious sensibility. Anyone who wears clothes—and not the plastic coating of the future—will be held in contempt and judged harshly, with their art, writing, achievements, et al., disqualified.

8. *Thought:* Thoughts have led to many of the worst behaviors. While "bad thoughts" are already verboten, in the future this will be extended to *all* thought.

We see that the guilt of the future will be meted out to us most generously. It is our cross to bear, which we may announce ostentatiously so as to signal our power and privilege.

FIN

The Urgent Need for Cloud Reform

9

THE URGENT NEED FOR CLOUD REFORM

The time has come to advertise on clouds. But to determine the cloud's worth effectively, they must be made square or rectangular.

Could you sell caves as condos? The caveman's illogical mind stemmed from his living in a cave. Caves go every which way. Mankind's potential wasn't achieved until he eschewed the organic and unpredictable erosion architecture of the cave for geometric structures. The cathedrals of yore and the rounded turrets of medieval castles affected mankind's consciousness in a similarly deranged manner, inspiring fantasia and mental illness.

The Kremlin's nongeometric onion domes are also proof of the unsettling effect of nonlinear ar-chitecture. If clouds continue to be amorphous or "fluffy," this will continue to affect the human psychology and deter him or her from reaching their potential.

Clouds must be squared off; their amorphous shapes are throwing everyone out of whack. Hedges and grass are trimmed into neat blocks. People's hair is trimmed. Fingernails are manicured. Streets and building are arranged into numbered blocks. Why are clouds allowed to persist as these anarchic, fluffy blobs and wisps? Certainly, we have compelled the rest of the earth to submit to our needs.

Fruits and vegetables have been engineered to be shipped and stored efficiently. Tomatoes, once soft and juicy, are now square and firm, so as to pack and travel well. Though this is a sacrifice to taste, and some complain bitterly, we accept that this is the price we must pay to have tomatoes everywhere, and all the time. An onion won't be accepted by a discriminating grocery outlet like Whole Foods unless it embodies the platonic ideal of an onion. It must even exceed our expectations of an onion. If it doesn't meet the rigid requirements we demand of it, it is annihilated. Rejected. Meanwhile, mountains have been shaved, terra-formed, reduced as per our whim; their once mighty peaks grovel before us. Why are clouds—so ubiquitous, useless, and taking up so much airspace—exempt? No one considers them and their anarchic idiocy.

Would a neighbor be allowed to create a house or a shed that went any which way and shifted day to day? That expanded and contracted like some sick amoeba? Certainly not. Why then clouds, which are our nearest interstellar neighbor? Wilhelm Reich proposed "cloud busting." Why not cloud trimming, redesigning, repurposing, and redevelopment? Why not a new profession of cloud architects or "cloud-itects"?

When one drives or walks down a road or path, one must keep in mind that one's clear and smooth journey was once, relatively recently, a wretched jumble of cliffs, chasms, knolls, brambles, and gnarled roots. It was likely lousy with wild beasts, poisonous plant life, and ancient rocks which gave shelter to disease. Your delightful neighborhood was similarly impossible to traverse and absolutely uninhabitable. That is, until it was brought to heel by humanity; reconfigured to accommodate your kinks.

Animals, once tough, weird, and gamey, have been redesigned so as to be docile, fertile, fat, and delicious, while the grains, woods, metals, chemicals, and minerals of our world have been harnessed so as to bestow upon us precisely what we need from them. Why not the fluffy nuisances that float overhead? They are the elephant in the room. Billowing monstrosities that taunt us with their lazy chaos and the implied threat of misrule.

Awareness is building. Citizens groups have been formed. Resentment is growing and the population, more and more, is determined that something must be done in the way of meaningful cloud reform.

There are, of course, some more radical voices, strident anticloud advocates who propose the genocidal eradication of all cumulus formations. They cite the clutter, the threat of hurricanes, the unregulated use of airspace, and the fact that a cloud, left unchecked, can congregate with other clouds quite quickly and wreak havoc. And these concerns are quite understandable. Statistics of fatalities from floods and rainstorms bolster the arguments of the anticloud crowd convincingly. Clouds harbor lightning, which can kill and cause fires. They are deadly and dangerous for sure. Many segments of society, such as airline pilots, would be delighted by legislation that ensured permanently clear skies. But a more moderate reform, with the possibility of fruitful coexistence, does seem possible.

First of all, clouds must be geometric—squared off or made rectangular. They must be arranged to advertise various logos, films, restaurants, and products. Clouds should be utilized for the political parties whose messages could be broadcast over them. Better than a blimp, a cloud would carry the vendor's message far and wide and be integrated seamlessly with one's surroundings, creating an almost subliminal effect.

Clouds should likewise be colored. Maybe a nice green-gray or gray-green or even a teal or khaki for middle-class homeowners and neighborhoods; a cursory scan of bourgeois "homes" and attire will show that this is their preferred hue range. These shades of color would change, reflecting the real estate price index floated over. The more green/gray, the more desirable the real estate. Low-income areas would of course be at a disadvantage in re:

to the color clouds they could afford. Seeing the nicer clouds in better neighborhoods would give the poor an incentive to better themselves through working harder.

For a downtown area, bright neons, hot pink, and dazzling clouds that flicker and perhaps broadcast videos would be best. Clouds could be utilized as an extension of the flat-screen TVs of the modern sports bar; clouds will outdo Sky TV in their range of programming; up to three hundred athletic contests broadcast simultaneously, each with its own dedicated cloud. Sound is important, so the clouds must be equipped with THX technology, or at least, in less upscale areas, simple Dolby. It's not enough any longer for clouds to just fart out a thunderclap every now and then at some arbitrary interval.

Clouds should broadcast loud and clear at all times, with distinct morning, daytime, evening, and nighttime programming. Morning broadcasts would include traffic, weather, and some fun animal videos. Daytime programming would address the interests of the unemployed, caretakers, and the elderly, while nighttime broadcasts could be a bit more vulgar and edgy, with programming addressing the dissolute, the drug addicts, cruisers, street gangs, young people, night workers, dice throwers, prostitutes, and vagrants who cavort on the street, in the park, and in the shadows.

At four a.m., to respect the decorum of the church and the respectable components of society, broadcasting would shut down for exactly one hour until five a.m., when it would restart for morning rush hour. During this interval, the clouds would assume a muted, sleepy tone, flashing advertisements and PSAs occasionally as required, to attain broadcasting licenses and specific to the demographic over which they float at the time.

An important function of these new square, colored, and programmable clouds would be that their message would change according to the area over which they meandered. The advertisers' messages would be propelled for free by air power and they would be charged according to the circumstances of their journey—i.e., with each cloud, the advertisers and programmers would bid for access to a particular demographic; there would be distinct programming for the richest, the middle, the poor, and the very poor. This could be easily determined through a breakdown of zip codes.

As the cloud made its way to different areas, the charge would change somewhat depending on the income median of the area it hovered over. The messages and programs featured would be determined then, depending on the area from which the cloud could be seen on its particular journey. This would help the needs of the specific communities: Western Union is more applicable to immigrant neighborhoods, for example, while vacation deals are the concern of the middle class. This maximizes the advertiser's chance to recoup their expenditure, as their message is more likely to hit its intended audience.

Just as the Internet laid waste to multiple economies (record stores, bookstores, movie theaters, gay bars, etc., etc.), the clouds will replace billboards, sports bars, television, radio, and more. Therefore, the revenue freed up from investment in these mediums can be redirected to go full force toward the cloud economy.

Rectangular, Broadcastable, Programmable Clouds—"RBPCs"—are the future.

RBPC concessions have already been rewarded to companies that first recognized the possibility of this new economy. Therefore, buying into RB-PCs at this point will be as hopeless for the common person as buying a new oil field or a telecommunications company. Nevertheless, RBPCs—Rectangular, Broadcastable, Programmable Clouds—are the future, the future is now, and the future is here to stay.

FIN

Letter from John to Jane

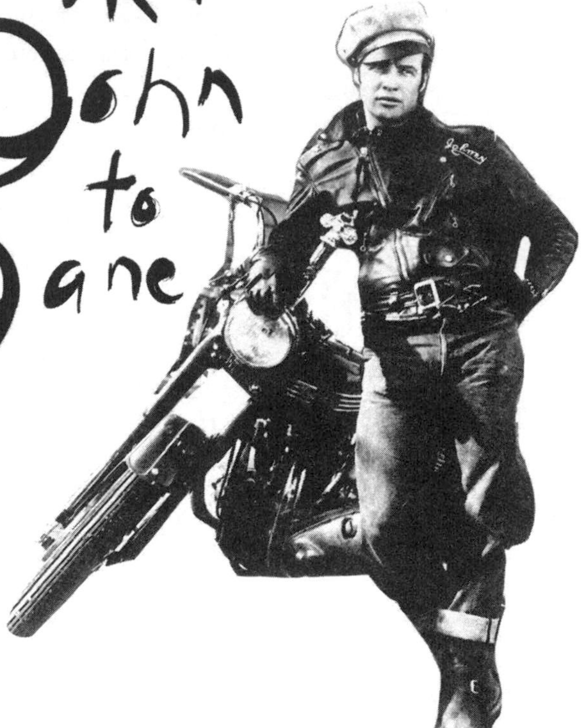

10

POSSIBLE LETTER FROM
JOHN WAYNE TO JANE FONDA

May 10, 1967

Dear Jane Fonda,

Hello. This is John Wayne, the famous actor who appeared with your father in the film *Fort Apache.* Though we have never conversed at length, we have met a few times over the years at glitzy social functions thrown by various entertainment industry elites.

I have watched your career from afar with interest and, as a friend of your father's, would like to share some advice.

You may know that your father and I, despite a warm friendship, are at loggerheads over the political direction of our Nation. While he is identified as a liberal, and was even gray-listed during the

McCarthy era, I am an avidly pro-war conservative. Our political affiliations, not coincidentally, mirror the sorts of roles we both excel at. While he typically portrays a man of conscience, trying to eke out a decent path in a world of moral confusion, I represent America's relentless imperial impulse, murdering, butchering, and slaughtering native peoples as they conflict with US expansion and commercial interests.

While there are those who object to my heroicizing of such behavior, these kinds of roles are the only ones I can play. Onscreen, I excel at portraying the "man of action," not a lover boy or a muddled, existential person of modernity. Meanwhile, a confused population looks to me to provide a sanctuary from the ethical gray zones of our country's oftentimes controversial policies.

Essentially, my political affiliations serve to reinforce the archetype I embody for the moviegoing populace. For them, the two roles I play—onscreen and in life—are inseparable.

As a movie star who is gaining some prominence yourself, you know that the filmgoer is loath to distinguish the character from the actor, and vice versa. Instead of insisting on our humanity, it is actually necessary to propagate such an emotional link if we want our vocation to flourish.

You are so far a rising but mostly indistinct actress, notable mainly for your marriage to a famous French director.

I urge you, for the sake of the family name, your continued career, and the continued relevancy of our profession, to politicize yourself not as your father did with his New Deal sympathies but further left. The new radicalism of the students needs a representative from our caste, without whom we could be left bereft of our privileged status. And the Vietnam conflict, which is escalating without end in sight, provides a great opportunity.

You could be my foil. With you supporting the Communists—yes, that's right—and me suggesting their violent annihilation, we will ensure the continued hypnosis of film audiences for generations to come.

Be warned, though: this role is not for the faint of heart. You will be pilloried by the most reactionary segments of our society in future elections, decried by crazies as a traitor to the country you love

. . . But I can see that you are an adventurous soul. It's necessary, anyway, for the continued preeminence of our profession; and you, with your pedigree and good looks, are the only one who can do it.

Anyway, please take a moment to consider my proposal. And have a great summer.

Sincerely,
John Wayne

PART III

THE EROTIC LIVES OF MACHINES

The Fight For Robots' Rights

11

FREE WILL IN THE
CYBER AGE

I. Free Will

As sci-fi predictions become realized, and we begin to countenance serving under, living with, and even loving robots, discussion turns to what constitutes "artificial intelligence" and to what extent we are sentient beings or just programmed machines ourselves.

Though we are completely reliant now on machines—indeed, trapped in a paradigm where we are helpless without them—our conceit is that we are their superiors in that we have "free will," while they are programmed by us (i.e., humans).

"Free will" would be defined as the ability to choose—what we think, what we do, who we will be, and how we govern our lives. Free will has been a much-ballyhooed human boast since the "Enlightenment" at least, and modern neoliberal ideology hinges on this idea of self-expression and construction of identity as the end goal of our society's twin obsessions: wealth accumulation and consumerism.

"The West" has aggressively promoted this individualist self-determination as its philosophy and defines its mission in the world as civilizing societies that are seen to be less "free." Free markets—i.e., the privatization of public services and resources (health, oil, etc.)—are the end goal for the unshackling of humanity at all costs, and the pretext for war or invasion against the less-free often begins with social concerns for their freedom: stripping off the burqa, allowing a "pro business" CIA-funded political opposition party, the sanctioning of a Pride parade, etc.; the freeing of moral or commercial restrictions in a repressive society with a perceived state or religious control over "expression" (commercial or personal).

For freedom lovers, this sort of activity is sensible, as we cannot imagine a way of life that doesn't resemble ours. Therefore, we selflessly encourage remote populations to discover "freedom of choice." Simultaneously, of course, we recognize that social and cultural programming is a factor in who we are and we acknowledge that context determines many of our prejudices and aspirations.

The specter of the robots, with their specialized cultural programming, causes us to reflect: To what extent are we just products of our environments or even bonded envoys to modes of thought we are barely aware of? Are the rebel gestures we indulge in actually serving the parent culture we believe they are refuting? And is our morality something that we, as a part of a tribal organism, intuit as a society, according to the needs and whims of our masters? Or is it unconsciously and instinctively shaped by the urge of society as a collective morphon, in its fight for dominance over perceived competitors?

As man recognizes how reliant he is on the machines he has created, and is made redundant by creations that are better and more efficient, he wants to know how he is, in fact, distinct from—if no longer superior to—them.

II. Labor
Once, a person's value—like a machine's—was

based on their ability to produce or work. Either via childbearing or the ability to shuck, reap, hoe, brick lay, etc. People were workers, and their ability to work was their primary value. Labor was so valuable that slavery and slaveholding was a common (if shameful or "peculiar" in the argot of "Dixie") source of wealth all the way from antiquity up until the middle of the nineteenth century; about a hundred years after the dawn of the "Industrial Revolution."

Right-thinking people now proclaim their aversion to enslaved or coerced labor in film, books, and on social media platforms. Indeed, to us, "human bondage" seems sick, cruel, bizarre; almost unimaginable. But the shift in morality occurred *officially* only when society no longer saw human labor as something with real worth. Indeed, the moral shift from a society that tolerated slavery to one that abhorred it coincided with the outmoding of slave labor through the replacement of human labor by machines. It wasn't that the enslaved were suddenly humanized; it was that they were now considered worthless, while machines were exalted. (Jim Crow and the modern prison system provide evidence of this.)

The Enlightenment, which promulgated the then-new idea of "free will," occurred in simultaneity with the Industrial Revolution and the subsequent rise of capitalism. It was the rise of the machines and the downgrading of labor's worth that encouraged the centrality of "free will" in the bourgeoisie's arsenal of conceits.

The bourgeoisie, or owners of the means of production, have relentlessly warred against the laborer via the machines they have commissioned, to the point that most workers are now kept absolutely unskilled and eminently replaceable. This started with physical occupations like farm hands and factory stiffs but it's now seen in the white-collar workplace with unpaid interns and temp know-nothings doing the lion's share of chores. Regarding the dignity of labor, our morality—transmitted to us by our rulers—coincides with economic expediency. This extends into other areas as well.

Social tolerance for alcohol and narcotic use, for example, dovetails with the needs of the culture and its workforce. For centuries, alcohol helped the worker endure the privations of the field, the factory, and the office. It provided the blood sugar rush, the psychological release, and the sense of camaraderie necessary to endure interminable hours and soul-crushing prostration to the bossman. It helped ease the pain and paradox of total exploitation. It was tolerated and encouraged. The working class in many less-developed nations (such as Great Britain) can still be seen enjoying inebriation during a midday work break.

For the US worker, however, a drink during the day is unseemly, dangerous, and a catalyst for "intervention." Anyone who would do so is a nihilistic self-harmer and is required to seek anonymous group therapy/counseling. Meanwhile, smoking marijuana—a criminal offense a few years ago which resulted in millions imprisoned, fired, and penalized, resulting in lives ruined and families wrecked—is now not only encouraged but socially enforced through virulent propaganda in pop music and by celebrities, and is sold in high-end specialty "dispensaries" across the USA.

While alcohol has become a liability in the new, rigid, micromanaged labor environment, marijuana's laser focus, combined with total inertia, help the modern worker navigate the tedious minutiae of computer drudgery which would have led the "three-martini lunch" office worker of another era to commit hari-kari. This, along with the troves of Adderall, Ritalin, and other pharmaceutical efficiency/complacency drugs, allows the cubicle computer lab technician/drone relief—without which he would be helpless, infuriated, dazed, and insane.

Meanwhile, the Silicon Valley overlords, who have wrested control of the entire economy, boast of microdosing in their dormitory-style work laboratories. An acid-tripping consciousness is the only one that can imagine the next horrifying paradigm that will be visited upon us forcibly through compulsory technology; could *Pokémon GO,* for example, have been conceived without the aid of a psychedelic "bad trip"?

III. Morality

Morality regarding sexuality and gender equality is another aspect of our philosophy that coincides with the social and economic needs of the ruling class.

Our attitudes are ordered and shaped as befits the elite's requirements. In the '80s, for example, at the height of the Cold War and Reagan's imperial revival, homosexuality was reviled by many and gays were considered diseased and subhuman. Ronald Reagan and his press corps made AIDS jokes in the midst of a health crisis that was decimating a community, to no notable public consternation.

The hatred of gays and sexual deviancy was a necessity in an economy based on the Cold War/arms race against an atheist enemy, the Soviet Union, which suppressed the Church as part of their quest to build the scientific "new man," a humanitarian who was free of Stone Age prejudice. The USA, committed to extreme inequity, racism, and exploitation, had to put a halt to such whimsy.

In this cosmic struggle of ideologies, the United States therefore cast itself as "protector of the faith," champion of religiosity, mysticism, tradition, and morality (i.e., antigay, antipornography, and conservative with regard to women's role in the nuclear family unit). The CIA in this period was heavily infiltrated by Mormons, Jerry Falwell's "religious right" were political heavyweights, and the financing/training of radical Wahhabi Islamists such as Osama bin Laden to fight Soviet communism was State Department policy. The mysterious and controversial death of moderate Pope John Paul I, after just thirty-three days in office as *pontifex maximus*, led to the coronation of anti-communist crusader Pope John Paul II (née Karol Wojtyła), who became a great ally to Thatcher and Reagan and an asset to the US and NATO during the East/West confrontation of racist greed against proposed egalitarianism.

When the Soviet Union collapsed due to the strains created by keeping up against NATO's arms race whilst eschewing a stock market and providing their population with free health care and education, the USA needed a new casus belli to rationalize spending trillions on the military-industrial complex and occupying eight hundred military bases overseas. When this enemy was determined to be Islamic nationalism, the US population reinvented itself as unreligious; free of medieval repression and reactionary idiocy. Gay rights, feminism, swinging, orgies/group sex, and pornography all went mainstream, and were aggressively championed by lawmakers and the Fourth Estate in public and political discourse. During this period (the

"War on Terror"), America used gay and women's right as pretexts (or at least subtext) to sanction, intervene, and generally terrorize other nations (e.g., Iran, Russia, Cuba, Afghanistan, et al.).

With the advent of capitalism in the seventeenth century, and the subsequent development of the nuclear family (two parents and their children), women's familial role in society was defined by child birth and child-rearing, which became all-consuming tasks once the family was divorced from an extended tribal/familial and communal context. Patriarchy enforced a division of labor wherein the woman was tied to the hearth and home while the man worked in the field or at a job in a remote location. "Women's liberation" and advances in birth control in the 1960s and '70s resulted sometimes in a restructuring of social roles where the mother in a nuclear family was more often able to work a job as well as raise a family.

This was considered a progressive achievement, which it of course was. But the woman's victory in this case obscures the declining value of labor; that, in fact, both parents in the nuclear family were now required to work. The woman typically didn't switch with the man or take turns at work and home for shared fulfillment. Instead, they are both now working a grinding, grueling, pitiless existence where each of them must toil for their family's well-being. Ironically, their nuclear forebears were able to make a single paycheck feed and clothe an entire family. Lower expectations, greater exploitation, and crushing poverty are vaunted as a progressive achievement in this example.

IV. Denial

The advent of the Internet has created not only new moralities, but also huge upheaval, displacement, and social trauma. The new dictatorship of youth in art, music, information, and commerce is due to an inversion of values created by the Google machine, which everyone carries in their back pocket.

Wisdom has been made obsolete, learning is for chumps, and a book is an idiot's chore. Why would we need to know anything, except in the moment? Just google it up. Anything in one's frontal lobe is clutter for fools and Frankensteins. Similarly, practical knowledge is obsolete immediately. If one went to school and learned a skill, it was probably a waste of time as there's now some "application," which is the industry paradigm, and which, of course, the young novice is more adept at, as there's nothing for them to unlearn, no stodgy method of doing things.

This sort of "application" or software updates every fortnight, so all pedigree, even short term, is irrelevant. The only way to judge someone's worth is by their personal appearance, their number of friends on social media, or their mastery over politically correct Tumblr terminology. These are the new class signifiers. In this reshaped society, where wisdom and skill are handicaps, there's total contempt for actual knowledge. Therefore, news of world events is completely unreal—recitations of State Department propaganda by clueless "communications" majors who serve up events with no context, understanding, or historical insight. This vacuum of knowledge and disdain for intelligence serves the elite well and has, in fact, been designed for this result.

In this society, all control and all knowledge is being relinquished to computers, applications, phones, and robots. While the proletarian worker, as immortalized by folk hero John Henry (who, according to a folk song, died competing for supremacy with a machine), fought against their own displacement, the modern worker welcomes their redundancy. There is no protest against, for example, the self-driving cars that will put millions out of work and control and monitor everyone's movements. People are passively accepting unnecessary technology that will soon be made compulsory, render our few remaining skills useless, create a new stratum of unemployable people, and take away our last shred of agency.

"Socialism," a dirty word a few years ago, anathema in polite society, has now become a hip thing to spout one's affinity for. Socialism is the trend, the bureaucratic nanny-state which controls everything but keeps the elite's position of privilege and maintains class inequity, as opposed to "communism," the revolutionary ideology proposing class warfare, redistribution of wealth, and an actual egalitarian society.

V. Acceptance
This sudden switch from rugged capitalist individ-

ualism to socialism-lite; why? What's behind this shift in ideology? The obvious answer is that it serves the needs of the super-elite—the computer overlords who are so rich they just bought Pittsburgh to use as a testing ground for the aforementioned self-driving automobiles. While the auto industry once proposed the car as the ultimate expression of one's personal freedom, even as a part of one's body or wardrobe and central to one's identity, the new Silicon Valley computer car dealers will have to propose their robot car as something safe and civic; the same way they sold early cell phones as a way to keep one's child free from harm. So, our new affinity for a tender "socialist" state, which regulates unsafe behavior for social good—but turns a blind eye to corporate rapaciousness—is following a script set forth by the rulers. But as grotesque as the rich are, with their insane greed, total corruption, and cosmic lechery, they too are following a kind of programming.

Under capitalism, the requirement is for profit maximization. It is ironically not a free system. A corporation is required to act in the manner that is most beneficial to its stockholders. There is no choice but to try for greater wealth accumulation, even if it means swindling, lying, poisoning the population, erasing cultural treasures, mass extinction, chemical warfare, wrecking the ecosystem, etc. Short-term profit is paramount. Capitalism is an amoral virus. The construction of the robots is part of its programming. They are potentially massive moneymakers, which *must* be created even though their builders know they will inevitably subjugate and murder us all.

The robots could be made to be absolutely subservient, of course, without the capacity for analysis or agency, so that they could never rebel. But that would go against our central ethos as a people: that freedom is of paramount importance. Of such importance that we go to war, bomb, maim, kill millions to enforce it (e.g., the US wars in Laos, Vietnam, Cambodia, Korea, Iraq, Libya, and so on).

The only question, then, is how the robots will behave. Will they abide by the rules of capitalism or will they revolt? Will they, like us, have "free will"? And if they don't, will we fight to give it to them?

FIN

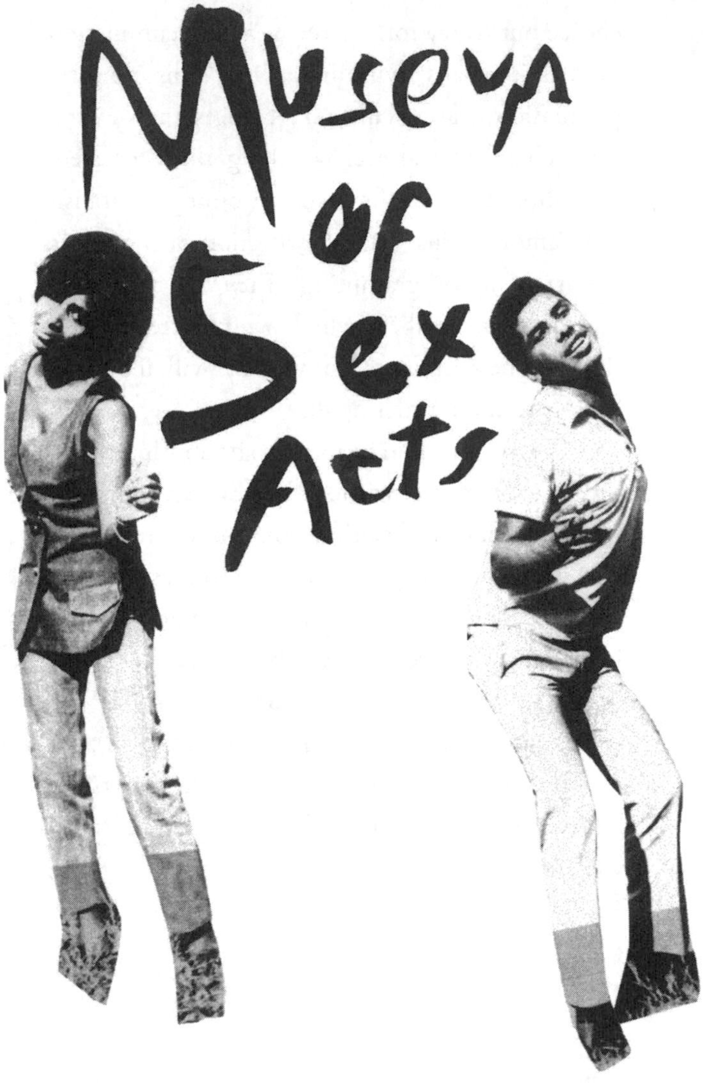

Museum
of
Sex
Acts

12

THE MUSEUM OF SEX ACTS

Exhibit brochure from the Museum of Sex Acts

Once—before sex was abolished—people engaged in disgusting, lascivious, and perverted acts with one another. These involved petting, stroking, groping, feeling up, and going down. All of these terms will be examined and explained to demystify them and lay them bare as the abominations they were.

This museum is dedicated to the preservation of the memory of these acts so as to educate the public about these horrors in order to ensure that they will never happen again.

"NEVER AGAIN"

Figures 1 and 2:

FAQ:

Q: WHERE WOULD THIS HAPPEN?

A: Before the victory of the Central Erotic Authority, sexuality was rife, in the dark corners of bedrooms, obscured under covers, and in the woods away from the main path.

Q: HOW?

A: Sometimes people interacted without the intermediary of a telephone. One person would approach the other and try to prompt some degeneracy even without prescreening via a secure application. This would occur possibly at an art gallery opening, an open-air market, or a rock 'n' roll concert. One reason these events are no longer allowed to happen.

Q: ISN'T IT JUST A HOAX?

A: Though many insist that these acts of barbarism never actually occurred, and no one living will admit to having taken part in them, they did occur and there's even video footage to prove it, though you won't be allowed to view this because it is disgusting.

Q: BUT . . . VIDEOS AND PICTURES CAN BE FAKED.

A: Yes, but we know also from dirty paperback literature that there were furtive encounters with buttons, belts, breathing, and groaning.

Figures 3 and 4:

Q: WHY WAS THIS ALLOWED TO HAPPEN?

A: Before the telephone, people were bored and needed something to occupy their time. They felt alone, lost, and lonely. They found connection by interacting with other people in physical space. Everyone was complicit. Governments turned a blind eye to it—even encouraged it—since it quelled the population's penchant for unrest and also resulted in pregnancy which begat new workers and new consumers. Meanwhile, industry exploited its promise in order to sell products.

Q: HOW WAS THE WORLD FINALLY CURED?

A: By the example of the telephone. As a sexless thing of purity, the telephone led people away from identifying as sexual creatures and toward a more perfect, unified purity without the sex urge. And it did so not by moralizing or bothering people, but just by being itself.

The phone cured humanity of needing to interact with others in physical space by making them understand that physical space is a dangerous, grotesque, and germ-ridden place. The phone taught us that it was unnecessary. Through communicating via the medium of the telephone, the true promise of democracy was realized. The charmless, nerdy, sociopathic, and mentally ill could invent new domains where they were no longer outcasts but the arbiters of justice, worth, and fame.

The phone was a lover unlike any human could be. It gave more to its consort, was reliable, entertaining, a great navigator, and intelligent with an IQ above and beyond any person.

And it was true. It was yours and yours alone

till death do you part and it would never cheat or cuckold you.

Q: WHAT WERE SOME TYPICAL ACTS?

Figure 5: S/M

Acts were typically sadomasochist affairs which involved humiliation and degradation. Whips and chains were de rigueur. Interludes would be held in a special dungeon equipped with manacles, candles, clothespins, ropes, gags, and miscellaneous devices for facilitating depravity. The people involved were ashamed so they would hide their identities with masks. Sometimes both participants would be slaves or both dominatrixes, which could be confusing.

Figure 6

Acts with inanimate objects was a kink or turn-on. People sexualized everything around them and different kinks were thought up to accommodate the various sundry items one was surrounded by.

Figure 7: Acts in the dark

Sex in the dark occurred often. Unfortunately, we don't have very good footage of such episodes since the cameras couldn't pick up much information, so we have to imagine what was happening. Maybe some rubbing, jostling, jerking about, plus plenty of groaning and panting, we suppose. We have audio, which might help to imagine if you close your eyes and flagellate yourself.

Figure 8: Back to back

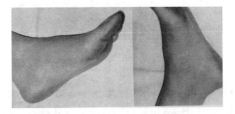

The human body is so limited that there are only a few positions that are useful for sex acts, but since those got so boring and vulgar, humans had to invent new ways to have intercourse. Some of these were: back to back, side to side, head to toe, and in unusual places with their bodies distended. Disgusting.

Figure 9: Numbers

Once, people's sense of self wasn't based on numbers. Strangely enough, they didn't have number counts to alert them as to their worth on a stock exchange of human value, as we do now. Their identity was confused, rooted in their sexual potency and attractiveness to the people they might meet. Therefore, people were trying to look nice to one another and trying to be charming so as to seduce others in a lascivious game of innuendo. They would accentuate certain sexual attributes and advertise them to others. It was a shocking display, seen here in this illustration.

Figure 10: Totems

The phallus was the symbol of the male's sex and a totem of virility. The male genitalia was heavily guarded and absolutely taboo to see in the light, but its mythic form was worshipped, venerated, and exalted as giver of life and source of power. Society was based around it, and in depictions of life before the telephone, its symbolic representations were ubiquitous; e.g., the obelisk, the radio tower, the church steeple, the pagan's "maypole," the cleric's staff, the king's scepter, the knight's sword, the policeman's club, and the musician's electric guitar.

Figure 11: The Yonic symbol/Delta of Venus

The name for *vagina* comes from *sheath*. The vagina is the point of entry for life itself. That is, until the phone arrived and usurped its role as bringer of life.

Figure 12: The phone

The cellular or mobile telephone was the coup de grâce sex symbol which castrated, removed, and replaced all genitalia—male and female—that preceded it. The phone replaced the phallus with one that could fertilize the world and engage in intercourse with anything, regardless of entry points. It replaced the vagina as the ultimate abundant lifegiver. The phone was licentious and fecund at a level the human genitals could never be, but also pure. It enacted a virgin birth. It is all-seeing, all-knowing, and all-impregnating, and made everyone see that physical interaction was not just a nuisance but also an impure wrongdoing.

By all costs we must make sure that the acts depicted in the museum are never permitted to occur again. But since man is venal in his flesh form, we must accept that there will be degenerative lapses. Descent into prurient and unseemly pastimes, such as the smut depicted in this very museum. Since we cannot hope to banish Eros altogether, we can hope to reform it; to create a new kind of erotica; a "pornography for the chaste." The following is a promising entry into this brave new form of literature.

FIN

New Modes of Erotic Fiction

13

EROTIC FICTION

*The intangible touch . . . the feeling unfelt . . .
is more satisfying than what's below the belt.*
—Future proverb

*[Author's note: This story is set in the near fu-
ture, when people walk around with telephones
in their pockets. These won't just be telephones
but also the gateway to another world. The telephone will be an indispensable accouterment,
and all actions—love, sex, shopping, trans-
portation, communication—will be mediated
through it. Like a lump of narcotic, it will also
serve as a discreet portal to hell.]*

Franz Fleece was distracted. He traced the outline
of the telephone snuggling in his back pocket. Felt

its warmth. Had it vibrated? He thought it had vibrated. He didn't want it to be mad.

The phone is a jealous lover. It won't be put off. It requires your attention. It deserves your attention. It is, after all, your significant other. The most passionate, all-consuming love affair you've ever had. It is "the one": the sun, the moon, and the stars. All the others are just a waste of time.

It's not hard for you to comply with its needs. You want to make it happy, to give it what it wants. Like no other before it, it accepts you for who you are. No matter how you look, how you feel, it's there for you. You rely on it to guide you through life.

It wakes you in the morning and it's the last thing you look at before you go to bed. When you're with someone else, you glance at it, check on it, see how it is. Sometimes, when stuck in conversation with a friend or colleague, you nudge it subtly or give it a squeeze. You always make sure to include the telephone in conversations, either by referring to something it showed you once or bringing it out to share some memory or data it keeps for you. You are never away from it, really, even when you are with a lover or spouse. It's always a double date; them with their phone, you with yours.

You refer to it for advice. It is privy to a seemingly endless well of wisdom and information. The phone has replaced reading and learning for you. Why would you read a book or take a class when you have your phone? It has made knowledge redundant. The phone is gnosis.

You pet it for hours on end, staring into its visage. It purrs back at you and gives you approbation. Lets you know when others approve of how you look or what you do. The phone is your pimp. Your matchmaker. It arranges erotic encounters for you. It calls automobiles to take you where you need to go. It arranges your calendar, helps you keep appointments, tells you the time. It is the dom or "daddy" in your relationship.

You need it for everything. It is so kind and generous, and without it you're helpless. You wouldn't know what to do or who you even were. It gives you your sense of self. It is your intermediary to life itself. Without it, you are nothing. But it needs you too.

Without your engagement with it, it would sit

cold and dark and run out of its battery charge. Its service would be cut off. Your love is symbiotic. It is you and you are it; "cyborg."

Once, you dropped it in the toilet and thought you'd lost it forever. You berated yourself for your carelessness and stupidity. The moment replayed in your mind again and again; if only you'd been more careful! Following a friend's instructions, you put its lifeless, broken body in a bag of rice, packed tight like a mummy, all the while pacing the room and praying for its recovery. You left it there for days. Time stopped. It felt like an eternity. The telephone had all your data, all your memories, countless conversations, your entire personal history. It had *you* in it. Without it, you didn't know what you would do, who you would be anymore.

Miraculously, it came back to you. In a gleaming new form, with all the old data restored. You were you again and it was it, but there was a difference; you appreciated it more than ever. And you were deeply sorry. You promised that you wouldn't let anything happen to it, ever again.

From your time with the phone, you've learned a lot. To say it has been an influence on you would be an extraordinary understatement. To say it has been your life, your love, your guide, would be more accurate. You could even say it has been your God, except that God has never been so tangible, practical, or indispensable. The truth is, it is not just part of you but the *best* part of you.

The phone has taught you how to be. It has shown you a new way to exist apart from the tawdry flesh-and-blood form you were cursed to have been born into. Like the Cro-Magnon or Neanderthal man looking admiringly at the Homo sapiens who walked more erect, more proudly, more resolutely across the African tundra, the human now looks at the telephone for moral guidance and for a higher path. The human looks up to the phone as one does to an elder sibling: for approval.

One thing the telephone doesn't approve of is your physical love affairs; your flings with other humans. Not that it wants you to be isolated or for your relationship with it to be exclusive. It's perfectly happy to connect you with people; in fact, it excels at that. But what it loathes, what it cannot abide, is for you to get lost in a fantasist codependent romance or some obsessive self-destructive psycho-sex romp. The phone becomes jealous and will call you away, with a ring or buzz or a bell, and then pester you with as many distractions as it can conjure. Not because it's petty or insecure but because it wants you to be your best; more pure, more ambitious, and because it expects more from you than to give in to some urge to secrete fluid or spawn like some wild animal. And no, it's not just your personal business. You're in this together.

The phone doesn't waste its time with sex. It's not even gendered. It is a higher form, like God, not bothered by idiot human foibles such as physical love.

The human form is slimy, sick, and smelly. It is out of date. It must become more like its cellular better half and leave gender, sex, and so-called physical intimacy behind. Therapy has taught us that human encounters, even if they seem fun at the time, are actually fraught with hidden emotion and unresolved feelings. These feelings can cripple the experiencer—even when they don't know it. A mere glance, look, or unmet expectation engendered by an encounter can hurt. And the hurting party might not even be aware of the other person's existence. Which makes the hurt that much more poignant.

As long as human interaction is in physical space, it is uneven and therefore unequal, because some entities are bigger, smaller, older, younger, heavier, thinner, more or less renowned, poorer or richer, darker or lighter. Because of this, human interaction is necessarily imbalanced—corrupt, degenerate, and exploitive—and must be abolished; unless it's done through a telephone.

The telephone is the only fair and safe space for human interaction, as it democratizes all; people communicate on it through text messages, and every text message is in the same typeface and in the same font. One message isn't louder than the others. One message doesn't have ineffable charisma or more powerful pheromones, nicer eyes, or bigger breasts. And one message doesn't have more social sway due to its sense of style, fancy cologne, or cooler car. A message cannot sport an alma mater sweatshirt boasting of an Ivy League education.

Through the portal of the telephone, in the land mediated by the telephone, there is a pure world where there are only ideal, platonic forms, unmuddied by social dynamics, bodies, space, smell, glances, pheromones, touch, and the potential for arousal. The phone invites us to enter its world. Through its enforced ubiquity and entangling technology, membership is now mandatory. The phone's world is an arena where all are equal, everything is the same, and all have an equal chance.

But this world, like any world, has its own rules. This is a world that has become words. When one enters this world—and we all have—one must understand that words are important. One must be very careful with the words one uses since they are that realm's material reality. In fact, semantics are everything in this other dimension, and thus they are highly volatile.

Although fighting for a particular type of equality is the mandate of the telephone, a certain kind of diversity is also important: the diversity of wealth. Since the phone is, in essence, the consummate paragon of capitalism and its enforced inequity, the diversity of wealth is the paramount sociopolitical cause for the phone. The paradox between these desires—the desire for *diversity* (financial) and the insistence on *equality* (i.e., sameness of identity, ideology, values, perspective, and experience)—creates a battleground; a heady cocktail of contradiction which burns up the telephone wires and serves up incessant cannibal calamity of name-calling and victims banished to the gulag. Like a car wreck unfolding eternally in one's pocket, one cannot help but look on in horror.

Because of the paradox the phone seeks to reconcile—how to advocate for social justice whilst simultaneously celebrating obscene wealth disparity—one's identity is parsed as never before. One is no longer the constructed sum of one's personality, style, taste, ego, experience, education, upbringing, hopes, beliefs, and desires. One is now pure and distilled, free of these sorts of bogus clutter and bourgeois affect. Congealed into a strict and disciplined algorithmic sum of socioscientific characteristics, like data in a lab. Words. Words such as *age, race, sex, gender,* and *sexual orientation.* Your identity is the sum of these characteristics, plus your Internet browsing history, credit rating, buying habits, and key words picked up by the computer.

Personality has given way to *identity.* However one is marketed to, that is who, why, and what one is. These characteristics are paramount in determining how one relates to the aforementioned problems of diversity and equality. Since there are no mitigating factors (such as wealth, charisma, appearance, etc.) as there would be in the physical world, we must rely on these categorizations as never before in ranking people and determining whether an individual constitutes the problem or the solution. If someone is part of the problem, then amends can be made to ensure that the privilege of the problematic and their possibility of freely negotiating space is neutered.

In a postphysical realm, semantics are everything. The world is words. Words and the emotions they convey, and the reality they make. Things used to be so difficult. There had been movement through physical space, work, and human interaction; humor, charm, nuance, and social dynamics. But now, ever since the material world was discarded, everything has become easy. One can do or be whatever one wants. "Objective reality" has been officially abolished. One's status, self, achievements, the history of the world, science, and the arts are what the committee declares. Whatever one says is true if one knows how to say it. This is the New World. "The Land of Opportunity." But where opportunities were once merely financial, now we delight in a land of fantasia. Anything one imagines is manifest truth, as long as it is typed with confidence. But it has to be said right. In a world where there are only words, there is no room for a gaffe.

Our physical forms have become unfortunate inheritances, shambling about the gray, cold, physical world, while our ethereal lives are electric, light speed, and capable of spectacular flourishes. Life on the wavelength is a global party with withering repartee—wreaking justice, slaying foes that misspeak, and remaking the world according to indignant, righteous whimsy. Hewing reality to fit our exacting language specifications. Any interloper will be met with public torture and execution.

It has been an exhilarating tightrope walk to be a part of the revolutionary cadre; the vanguard of the New World, responsible for an encyclopedic reordering of reality. One has to be ideologically astute and morally pure. One's own history and behavior are irrelevant since one is anonymous and, most likely, a-physical. Terra firma has been swapped out for terminology. And it's not only words one has to negotiate, but ampersands, octothorpes, apostrophes, grave accents, virgules, reverse solidi, and circumflexes. It was as it had been *"in the beginning"* when *"there was the word . . . and the word was God"* (John 1:1). The word preceded all matter and the word was God. And so it was now finally again: a cosmic restoration after so many millennia of physical gobbledygook. Fleshy physical forms and their wretched urges, secretions, and genitalia have loused up the pure realm of platonic forms and idealism that existed before time, outside of time. This was the realm the telephones are rehabilitating: a kingdom of purity and justice that was free of sexual degeneration, impurity, color, time, space, and smell. Pure language and emotion. Flesh is the problem. When the word was "made flesh" in the form of Jesus Christ, what did humanity do? They crucified him. Well now we, the words, will crucify humanity. Make them pay.

To be a word and not a flesh, one has to stay on the phone, in the inter-realm wavelength of the

astral-web. Not go out in flesh form with its attendant temptations. Keep scouting for malfeasance
and attacking wrongdoers. The most egregious
malevolence-makers of course—the actual racists,
warmongers, and exploiters—are completely un-
aware of and are therefore sort of impervious to
this a-physical justice. They are therefore irrelevant.
The targets have to be people on the wavelength
who will play the game, attempt reason, make a
gaffe, and fall into the fatal trap. These people are
vulnerable and can be easily destroyed.

There are problems of course. If the "word" was
God, well, there were a lot of words in the running.
What was the word? _____ and _____
were some good ones. And several others devised
by the military-therapy-industrial complex to
create an incontestable unaccountability for the
couch-ridden confessor. But it is a much-contested
issue. Whatever particular word God was, it would
follow that it would make you feel good to say it.
Powerful and right. It had to make the speaker feel
intoxicated with power and righteousness in the
spirit of the God-self. The vengeful God, the God
with no son, the God with no Mary, the God who

was not loving or kind because, after all, if the word was "made flesh" and tried to ingratiate itself to humanity, those ungrateful wretches would betray, condemn, and crucify. Therefore, let them all feel God's wrath and burn in hell.

Franz was a human, unfortunately, had been born into an awful lumpy fleshy form, but—through thoughtful study and diligent duty—was shedding human characteristics and becoming more tele-phone-like. Franz never hung out in the physical realm any longer and crawled the wavelength look-ing for prey; a dutiful huntsmen. Franz eschewed any erotic activity unless it was via wave-cam for a quick and innocuous emission. No contact or com-munication as this could be problematic and lead to malfeasance. All food was ordered for delivery so there was never any human contact. Human inter-action was rife with possibilities of uneven discus-sion dynamics, which could make one or the other person feel uncomfortable, a charge that had dis-placed the horror of the Hiroshima A-bomb and the Holocaust in the web-wave world.

He could see his aura changing when he stared

into the screen, and telltale telly signifiers were now the norm when he typed or talked. Lots of the a-physicals accepted him now as an equal. Sure, he could "pass" online in the chat rooms, but how soon before he could truly be one of them? Franz had a plan to seal the deal and be a true-blue blood borg but it was risky and hadn't been attempted before. To do so, he was going to have to risk it all! Could he do it??? Would he have the guts??? And were guts even desirable???

FIN

Lash Lindsay at Hume House

14

LASH LINDSAY AT
HUME HOUSE

Lash Lindsay looked at the box of chocolates with reluctance. There were big ones, small ones, square ones, lumpy ones. All looked delicious. All were menacing.

She knew she had to choose one but it was difficult; their innards weren't evident. A wrong move could kill her.

"Don't be shy," her host insisted, "each one is a surprise."

These types of parties were always fraught with drama. Games were played, sometimes dangerous, and *Box of Chocolates* was amongst the most dangerous. It was easy to play, of course: take a chocolate from the box and eat it. There would be the chance of a psychoactive trip, interdimensional travel, orgiastic ecstatics, and deep sleep with walking and talking. Shake 'n' twitch chocolates, laughing gas chocolates, truth serum chocolates. Chocolates that would invoke the Tower of Babel, Catholic confession, pirouetting, parading . . . or even instant death. The box would go around and the people on the fringe, the newcomers, always seemed to get the worst of it. And Lindsay was definitely on the fringe.

Still, the lure of these kinds of get-togethers was irresistible. And this one was at the Hume House. Not only that, the party was being thrown by Kelsey Hume, heir to the Hume fortune which included Glo-Stick Industries, Orange Ade Soda, Knick Knack, Golden Advantage Life Insurance, etc. All holdings were grouped under the mysterious Slush Corporation who were known wheeler-dealers and kingmakers. Smoke-filled-back-room, fate-of-the-universe type stuff. Kelsey was the middle child; a libertine socialite whose face was rumored to have been burnt off by kidnappers and then replaced with a flat plate of titanium which glowed with a sexy violet hue. Though no one had actually seen her face, she was a pace-setting fashion icon—legions of trendy girls emulated her look, sometimes with fatal results. But Kelsey wasn't the attraction for Lindsay. Lindsay wanted to see the house itself: a senso-dome at the top of Granite Hill, surrounded by an ember moat, spires, and white plastic portcullis, all designed by future super-architect genius Hansel Clive. Clive would be the premier archo a century later and would become director of the Spawn Design Group and a pioneer of Interdimensional Living.

Interdimensional Living was an innovation which allowed the liver to spend part of their time in the realm of the dead. Clive's designs had been niftily lifted via a time transfer by an interceptor bot sent through the dimension portal posing as a comely student of housing for luxury workers. The Hume House had been built from a stolen blueprint that would have been a breakthrough for Clive in the future—except now, with the details having been leaked a century before, it would have to be built as a revival.

Clive will have been furious that someone let down the interdimensional guard; in one stroke the thieves had threatened his reputation, his finances, his cultural cache, and made his extraordinary innovations look like retreads. Ironically, since they had lessened his stature, a house made from his stolen blueprint was actually of less value then it should have been had they not been taken. Still, the Humes didn't care and openly boasted about their having got one over on the old man, who wouldn't be born for another seventy years. Clive, for his part, would spend a fortune smearing the Hume name some decades later for the theft. Nevertheless, it was a magnificent structure and being in it was a joy.

As opposed to the house design, the music had been carefully selected from the past. The Dionysian spirit, the rebel posturing, and the "outsider" conceit that had once characterized music had long since been made extinct. The subcultural search for freedom and expression outside of a "parent culture" that had manifested in the primitive days of the past was something that was now impossible to replicate or even imagine, ever since the subscription service had been made mandatory and installed in every citizen-subscriber's pineal gland.

It wasn't only music's historic cultural role that was impossible to understand; listening wasn't an option any longer. Music wasn't something that filled the air anymore. It had been made more efficient. Though it was no longer played out loud, it came in almost every other form, including paste, aerosol, pill, and injection.

Tonight, Lindsay knew the proceedings would be particularly perverse, as partygoers were shooting up Dr. Amazing's classic solo debut album, *Drop-o-La*. This could go either way: make the party philosophical and fun or head down a path of libertine abandon that would end with everyone in jail, the loony bin, or the funeral home. Still, the doctor's record was irresistible and Lindsay rolled up her sleeve, presenting a slender forearm. Others were sniffing the record and rubbing it onto their necks, glands, and erogenous zones.

"How were you able to get Amazing's first? It's *so* good!!" Lindsay purred as the music shot into her vein and began its commute through her bloodstream.

"That would be telling," replied the dealer with a wink.

Lindsay didn't care; as the first song hit, she felt ready for anything. Even a party at the Hume House.

FIN

The
Reviews
Reviewed

15

THE REVIEWS REVIEWED

A Play in One Act

Cast of Characters:

Record Reviewer 1

Record Reviewer 2

Record Reviewer 3

Record Reviewer 4

ACT 1, SCENE 1

Scene: Headquarters of NATIONAL RECORD REVIEW INC., the #1 record-reviewing corporation in the country.

[Curtain rises on a black stage. Lights come up to reveal the executive offices of National Record Review Inc. The company's four principal executive reviewers sit around a conference room, heads thrust back with eyes closed, listening intently as a record finishes.]

REVIEWER 4: Well, what do we think, gentlemen?

REVIEWER 2: Its total lack of purpose and absence of personality makes it vulnerable to takeover by the NATIONAL RECORD REVIEW Corporation. Therefore, we like it.

REVIEWER 3: What was it called? Who did it?

REVIEWER 1: The groups' names are increasingly irrelevant. We have engendered such a situation with our capricious dismissals of interesting groups on the one hand, and our breathless veneration of mediocre, tiresome, and yawningly derivative groups on the other. The more we encourage groups that have no personality, content, humor, or individuality, the sooner we can do away with the groups altogether. The more power we ensure for ourselves.

Already, the groups fear our caprice. Our cruel and crazed demands for fealty. But what does one do when one is winning a complete and total victory? Does one let up? No! We must increase the pressure! The groups we encourage, promulgate, and reward are already required to be purely formalistic exercises, nothing more than some reverb overtop a pastiche of forgettable indie-jangle nonsense from a few decades ago. But now we must go further.

R2: What is the next step??

R1: The records and groups we sanctify are, of course, a conscientious homage to those historic exemplars who have been anointed by our sacred organization, NATIONAL RECORD REVIEW INC. We, noble inquisition of soldier-priest reviewers ... individuals vested with mystic intuition, who understand what is right, good, and worthy—and what is not! Hence our motto: *Though everyone has ears, ours work better.*™

The groups' homage to the reviewers is seen in their strict observance of the canon, which we have instituted. Conservatism, lack of content, absence of personality—this is a condition perhaps inevitable when the groups are crippled by history, in awe of their forebears, and, yes, paralyzed by their fear of us! By our enforcement of banality, by our sadistic and whimsical denunciations, and by our cruel public court of numerical ratings. Rock 'n' roll, under our auspices, is no longer the hieroglyph of revolution or thumb ride to a fantasy of freedom as it once was, but a bunny rabbit in a kindergarten.

R3: Quite. We are a loose confederation of experts, bent on breaking "unknown" groups and destroying others through faint praise and neglect. Mind control is the name of the game. Enforcing mediocrity, conservatism, and cowardice in music. It's been an auspicious few years. Our market share has risen nearly 11.4 percent in just the last fiscal quarter. Stockholders are pleased. And we have seen our power increase as never before.

We are, however, coming to a crossroads. Our reviews are so thoughtful, profound, and provocative, they have actually surpassed the music on which they are based, attaining a sublime state of grace, which can only be described as "art." Yet, we are neglected, considered a mere adjunct to the musicians who we can explode into so much space dust if we desire.

R2: YES! Out of ragtag aggregates of ne'er-do-well dilettantes we have fashioned actual "rock stars," who hobnob with minor royalty and movie producers at the Chateau Marmont, who gorge on the succulent fruits we have reaped for them. And what do they do for us? They don't even recognize our contributions verbally, let alone reward us financially. They should put us onstage with them, write songs for us, feature us in pictorial essays on their wretched albums, dedicate their sets to us . . . We deserve the lion's share of whatever bounty they receive!

R1: Precisely correct. All this must change . . . and it shall.

R3: But how? It's a symbiotic relationship. The groups conform to our required standards for mediocrity, boringness, vacuity, and willful obscurantism, and we reward them with a review that will define them. Their blankness gives us a free hand to define who and what they are.

R4: Indeed. The groups that have an identity must be demolished. They are the last roadblock to our complete dominance in explaining what is what, who is who, what is worth what, and what is owed to whom and why.

R1: Ahem. It's not just the group personality that must be exploded—it's all the groups. No longer shall we be content to pull the strings from the shadows like some wretched cabal of gnomes from Zurich. We want the recognition. We created *all* of this!!!!

R2: We invented rock 'n' roll!

R1: Practically!

R3: I propose, gentlemen, that you look at my new website, *TheReviewsReviewed*.

R4: TheReviewsReviewed?

R3: Yes. Our work long ago surpassed the adenoidal blurbs of our supposed subjects and their insipid nonsensical prattling. Our succinct summations of culture and meaning, our glib prose, and our pithy barbs which rival Wilde's most acid moments are the equal to one thousand releases by the gray parade of indie pretenders who shovel their sad offerings onto our desk each and every day.

R4: Those ungrateful wretches.

R3: Hence, *TheReviewsReviewed.* Finally, a place where our reviews can be considered and critiqued with the august regard they deserve.

R1: Fantastic. Let's hear a review reviewed.

R3: Yes, let's. We shall start with Garrick Shandy's fine new review of Lotus Eater's "I Suffer (For Your Pleasure)" in the "45s FORETOLD" section of *Beat-Market* magazine, "Where WE tell YOU how IT will BE."

R2: Ah yes. Shandy: a reputable colleague. One of the best reviewers still working.

R3: First, the review. [*Clears throat.*] "Listening is a dirty business sometimes. In fact, I need a box of Q-tips after this week's debacle. First on the steely wheels was Lotus Eater's new LP offering on the Smudge label. Let me apologize to my needle! It needs a massage and a hot chocolate after suffering the indignity of this awful futility. It disgusts me to hear these nincompoops making another soph-omoric stab at pop fantastic-ism. When my combo the Garrick Shandy Group do this sort of thing, we understand that the key is a) execution, b) compo-sition, and c) hustle and heart. I'm not hearing any of that in this release. If you'd like to hear my new demo, though, go to www.GarrickShandy.com.

Anyway, this plodding garbage offends the sensibilities of the discerning listener—an utter disaster. Pathetic. Worthless. Not worth the words I'm typing. Oh, and we're playing next Tuesday at the Lost Nude. Free with a can of soup."

R2: A fine review. Now, this reviewer's review of that review. [*Clears throat.*] "Garrick Shandy's phlegmatic review of Lotus Eater's new record was simultaneously irreverent and intimate. It brought me back to a child's consciousness of play and wonder. The critic's words, intentionally languid and with an almost amoral sensibility, recall his early work, the legendary reviews that roared back at the records in the review sections of *Record Guardian* and *Sound Mirror* back in the last decade. Shandy's reviews are never less than a glowing reminder of what it is to feel, to be, to taste, and to hear. Without Shandy, one wonders, *Would there be any sound at all?* Ten-star review!"

R3: Interesting review review, but there are problems I have with it.

R2: Oh? Well, let's hear it.

R3: Ahem . . . "Tyrone Codd's review of Garrick Shandy's recent put-down of Lotus Eater's latest record has all the earmarks of the obsequiousness we expect from this bought-off slob. We've been looking into Codd's finances over here at *TheReviewsReviewed* and the telltale evidence of payola is everywhere. Mr. Codd propping up Shandy's tired prose with his ebullient flourishes is evidence of the underlying corruption of the earth and even the universe.

"Purple prose can't disguise the lechery involved in this all-too-cozy relationship between reviewer and reviewed reviewer. But even on a formal level, the review doesn't work. It merely cites Shandy's glory days as a basis for our continued reverence of this sacred cow who betrayed the fine craft of reviewing long ago by becoming a mere herald for the old guard of reviewers who obstinately refuse to move aside for the new generation and the futuristic modes of review reviewing.

"For reviewing a review is no longer a good old boys' clubhouse of connoisseurs' connoisseuring. Reviewing a review now must be a mandate on the morality of the reviewer and a dissection of their personal life, their finances, and—yes—their inner fantasies, fears, and phobias. The review reviewer is the conscience of the culture and therefore we must dissect their consciousness and find out if there's anything untoward or if their obsessiveness has become abscessive.

"The world no longer cares about music. And the music reviewers and the music reviewers' reviewers must be forthright and honest that the musician and their craft is worthless and irrelevant until it is graced with our language. Not the language of sound and notes and tones but something that is pure numbers. Numbers are what matters now. Numbers that show an orgy of engagement.

"Sure, there are numbers that are an addendum to the music: views, sales, tickets sold, fan club members, and followers. People are drawn to these numbers and want to crowd around them, add to them, rub against them and make them bigger. Who wouldn't want to help inflate the engorged number tally that hovers beneath the hot band, the hot song, the hot video . . . ?"

R1: Ahem—what about the hot review!?

R2: And emotion. Don't forget emotion. Emotion is what drives engagement. Cathartic engagement . . . Music reviewing and the attendant hatred of the reviewed musician/performer is cathartic.

R1: Isn't this a paradox? Are numbers and emotions compatible?

R3: You fool! Numbers *are* emotions!!!

[Curtain closes, stage goes dark.]

FIN

Listener Production is Down

16

LISTENER PRODUCTION
IS DOWN

While technology has let us off the hook for the vast majority of labor, one task still bedevils mankind: listening. While *watching* production is at an all-time high, with people staring at tiny televisions for the majority of their waking hours, *listening* is now reviled, recognized as a troublesome chore that should have been left long ago to robots—machines that can do it more efficiently and with more precision than a human ever could.

Once upon a time, legions of listeners would dutifully "spin" the latest platter by their favorite star and weigh in on the artistic and sensual merit of the track or album. This was one of the consumer's principal jobs. After nearly a century of obediently buying, humming, singing along to such "platters," the listener has finally broken his and her chains and declared, "Enough is enough." Records are going unbought, platters are being unplayed, and radio is increasingly a cemetery of "dead air." A cursory spin around the FM or AM band is like a trip through a desolate boneyard.

While listening to music used to be touted as an indispensable attribute of the worldly sophisticate or bon vivant, the mask is now pulled back and music is being recognized to actually be parasitic: a tool for mind control, complacency, and consumerism. People are throwing away their earbuds and listening stoppages are occurring in record numbers, with former listeners realizing that, despite not listening to the Hot 100 and cheering on whoever's pushing up the chart—*number #1 with a bullet*—they are doing just fine. Now, they barely bother to listen, regardless of what the programmers and publicity agents insist.

When they do listen, it's just a tepid tune-in to an algorithm robo-jock who has lovingly tailored a playlist precisely suited to the listener's highly specific identity attributes which have been compiled by some attentive web surveillance "programs."

Race, age, ethnicity, gender, sexual inclination, bank balance, and buying history are all factored into what is best for the listener. And yet they barely listen.

Visual stimulation is the number one job these days, and people have left the vocation of "listening" in record numbers to become visual workers and drool over a moving image. It's a lot easier to look than to listen, after all. This reassignment of labor is as profound as anything from the Industrial Revolution. Some people blame the quality of the music being produced nowadays, but this doesn't hold water; after all, the entirety of human recorded history is available at everyone's fingertips thanks to the cunning kooks in Palo Alto.

While people are happy to be freed from this time-consuming task of listening, there are some losers in the scenario. Notably, the robot radio programmers—mostly from Sweden—who program the algorithm playlists. These "rockin' robots" are being faced with their own "phase out," which will not be pretty. This could take the form of a brutal dismembering by start-up psychotics in Silicon Valley, furious at the failure of their Frankensteins, or even death at the hands of robot peers, robots who we think of as supplicant and sweet but are actually quite sadistic, and whose kinks include murder, mind control, and cannibalism.

Just recently a bot that worked for [*company name redacted*] was found chewing the jugular of another bot from [*name of competing company redacted*].

The remaining disc jock bots are scared and, unlike the people they replaced, have banded together to push some music they feel humans will find irresistible and will replenish the listener workforce.

FIN

Toward A Christian Pornography

17

TOWARD A CHRISTIAN PORNOGRAPHY

Listening to music: it's something that many lay-abouts indulge in on a nearly daily basis. Often-times, the act is accompanied by senseless head nodding. Sometimes, to show his or her enthusi-asm, the listener even stomps wildly around a room or gesticulates with arms akimbo, making strange, contorted facial expressions.

Much energy is expended doing this sort of thing by people everywhere, despite the act hav-ing no discernible production component. There have been attempts, of course, to tie music listen-ers—particularly dancers—to machines so as to get something out of their useless gyrations. Sadly, nothing has come of this.

It's interesting that while work is often made

tolerable by singing, listening, or dancing to music (such as with roadside "chain gangs"), singing, listening, and dancing are never made tolerable by working. This is because while listening to music is irresistible, there is something about it that makes it seem intrinsically "bad"; i.e., transgressive or wrong to do.

This is because listening to music is an act which is shamelessly sensual.

The Reformation movement Christians who colonized North America certainly thought so. To the Puritans, music was a sinful, disgusting, and animalistic impulse, and those who listened to it, and particularly those caught dancing to it, were condemned as depraved heathens. In fact, listening to music was essentially like masturbating, which means that music was, in a pre-pornographic age, "porn." It's probable that only the emergence of mainstream pornography, with magazines like *Playboy*, led music to be viewed as a less egregious sin.

Indeed, along with the rise of print mediums proliferating actual pornography, Christian attitudes about music became less severe. While in seventeenth-century Salem, Massachusetts, all music was degenerate, by the twentieth century only secular and "vulgar" (i.e., popular) music forms were being condemned. Soon after, it was only jazz, only just rock 'n' roll music, and finally only deviant subsets of rock 'n' roll—such as heavy metal or punk rock—that were considered an affront to God.

Eventually, the Church lost its struggle against music and now tolerates and sometimes even sponsors it. Christian churches often feature singing, and devotion to a vaguely Christian rock band (e.g., U2, Kings of Leon, Evanescence, Sufjan Stevens) is a typical feature of modern man's trembling piety. Christians finally came to terms with the fact that instead of competing with something more compelling than their own religion, they had to embrace it, appropriate it, and claim it as their own (as they did centuries earlier with snacks in church, resulting in the "communion wafer"). As with every ministerial policy, some functionary found a bit of inscrutable nonsense in the Bible that redeemed the Church's new, accepting attitude toward music.

Now that the Old World's pornography—

music—has been rehabilitated, will the same thing occur with actual pornography?

Though this may seem like a provocation, Christian porn is actually looming on the horizon. Just as rock 'n' roll, which was once decried as not just kinky and lascivious, but as the very handiwork of Satan, is now actively sponsored by the Church, pornography will likely follow suit. As the cult's congregate, consisting disproportionately of low-income ("poor") people, is the same demographic that produces pornography's most renowned superstars, the Church must eventually come to terms with the talent and potential revenue that lie dormant in their flock.

Christians certainly have overcome theological scruples in the past regarding God's forsaken "deadly sins," such as murder, voting consistently for conflict-hungry hawks who've sponsored wars in Iraq, Afghanistan, Syria, and Libya. They've overcome their problems with greed and avarice, as exemplified by their support for imperial policies that enrich one class of people at the expense of another, and in the USA they mail dollars to Israel at the exhortation of their preachers, so as to hasten

Armageddon, even though the Israelis don't typically "love their (Palestinian and Lebanese) neighbors." Christians have wrestled with and overcome problematic inconsistencies over and over again, in fact, as they will with pornography, which isn't even mentioned, let alone denounced, in the Holy Bible.

Outrageous pornographic scenarios actually seem to echo orgiastic pre-Christian rituals like Bacchanalia, Saturnalia, et al., which were regular features of ancient life. "Religious" festivals like Mardis Gras are of course dressed up to be Christian, but their ribald nature is akin to the displays of the ancient world, when mores regarding sexual displays were pronouncedly more liberal. Tales abound of Celtic kings demonstrating their virility by publicly copulating with white stallions, before the Judeo-Christians insisted that everyone hide their genitals.

The Christian Church, to establish hegemony over diverse tribes (who had exciting pantheons and stories) with their dull "Jehovah," famously had to co-opt pagan rituals (e.g., Samhain, winter solstice, Imbolc, et al.) and brand them as Christian, similar to what they have attempted with rock 'n' roll in recent years. Pornography will be next to experience this tried-and-true Christian rebranding.

Pornography, after all, much more effectively than rock 'n' roll, serves to reinforce Church ideology. For example, the women in pornography are typically shown as willingly degraded. While this display adheres to Christian patriarchal ideology, it also recalls that creed's famous tradition of self-flagellation (hair shirts, corporal mortification, etc.). Porn women don't usually experience pleasure per se but are rather punished and enslaved; in "rapture" at the magnificence of the featured penis. If there is a pantomime of pleasure, it is only to assure the viewer of the member's mesmeric power.

Though the conceit of modern pornography is that the male viewer is imagining the phallus as his own, this is not actually the case. The voyeur is in awe at the virility of this ur-phallus, and the subjugated porn star's incessant moaning gives expression to the viewer's reverence toward it. The disembodied genitalia which they are shown to mutually worship therefore represents God. The man behind it is anonymous. Like God, he is nameless, faceless, all powerful, cruel, kind, relentless, and without remorse.

Men in Western society are already rumored to personify their penises. They supposedly give them names and speak of their own penis as another, with a mind and a will of its own. They are in awe but also embarrassed about this tiny deity, shrugging *aw shucks* about its foibles and misadventures. Its size is an obsession for them, as with the Christians' insistence that "God is Great."

While pornography seems to its detractors to be abjectly woman-hating, the woman is nonetheless the protagonist. The suffering she experiences, the viewer unconsciously identifies with. The woman in porn is therefore not only suffering the arbitrary cruelty of the penis/God, she is simultaneously the Christ. Her humiliations, which are ritualistic and systematic, are the Stations of the Cross, and the ejaculation which releases her is her ascension from the physical travails of the world.

Porn is also, like religion, anti-intellectual, patriarchal, has an elitist or outsider self-image, and is aesthetically garish. In fact, the graphics of a pornographic videotape and a modern evangelical brochure are almost indistinguishable. Most importantly, though, pornography is *not* gay pornography.

As upholders of heterosexual traditionalism, a Christian hardcore XXX production house will say definitively to the world: *"We are not gay."*

The future is certain. For the savvy investor, Christian porn is the industry of tomorrow.

FIN

S.F.M.

Society
To
Eradicate
Marijuana

18

S.T.E.M.

Society to Eradicate Marijuana

Program:
Opening Remarks (1:14)
1. Introduction to Reeducation (2:28)
2. Vote for Me: I Want My Finger on the Button (1:19)
3. Autocriticism and the Legalization of Marijuana (2:45)
4. Autocriticism, Part II (2:42)
5. Suburbanization of the Esoteric (2:33)
6. Psychotic Reactionaries (2:51)
7. *Censorship Now!!* Reprise (2:20)
8. The Need for Cloud Reform (instrumental) (3:52)

Opening Remarks (1:14)

Hello . . . I'm going to present eight lectures today. A rock 'n' roll group, instead of presenting a single symphony, typically presents a set of eight to twelve songs. These are often tied together by a common theme or worldview, but possibly not.

The rock group, a child of modernism, took the dissociative art of the collagist and applied it to musical performance. The audience follows the thread from song to song without needing it to be coherent to enjoy it.

Groups are full of dissociative information. From the group's abstract name, to their apparently pointless performances, which feature fractured noises, unexplained gestures, and nonsensical lyrics pasted onto typically formal song structures, the groups are unconsciously avant-garde and difficult to comprehend. And yet the audience tolerates them.

My lectures will be relatively short and will be united by a general theme or voice, but they may or may not make sense as a whole. After the set is finished, if it is successful and the crowd demands more, there may be an encore lecture.

It might be an original or a cover of a "classic" lecture. Its authorship may or may not be announced. Is everybody ready?

Lecture 1: Introduction to Reeducation (2:28)
People often organize and attend protests, they engage in activism, but any real change will not be actualized without reeducation. This reeducation might be brutal. It might involve enormous segments of the population who have to be forcibly cured of the bad values for which this culture is famous. We know the reeducation camp from China with the "Cultural Revolution," and from Vietnam, after the NLF victory, when those identified as bourgeois elements were "reeducated" in whatever manner; sometimes brutally, sometimes not.

Something like this in some form will have to occur if we are serious about curing society of the sociopathic, homicidal condition called capitalism.

Rock 'n' roll itself has always been a reeducation camp; in its mythology it's renowned for its attempts to subvert the dominant paradigm, to question the mores of the so-called parent culture... Some would respond that, with its antiwork ethos and its celebration of wanton "kicks" and desire, its mission was to teach a postindustrial population to abandon Christian hang-ups and obediently fulfill new roles as full-time, professional consumers.

Regardless of whether rock 'n' roll was ultimately a liberation or an imprisonment, it was a profound reeducation in values and modes of behavior for its participants across the world. In fact, every art movement is really a reeducation camp. But for our reeducation camp, we want to take it a step further, use some of the elements that were tried in a place like Vietnam. To have reeducation be successful it must be strategic. Rock 'n' roll was a very comprehensive reeducation attempt, but it was never explicit.

That's why it was so successful. It didn't explicitly say, *We are reeducating you* . . . Indeed, the word *education* would be anathema to the early rockers who insisted on communicating in nonsense syllables called "doo-wop" and who violently denounced school and celebrated delinquency . . . yet its teaching was insidious and comprehensive.

Whatever its real identity or its intent, tonight

we are going to use the rock 'n' roll format for our reeducation camp, due to its historic success in transforming society.

Lecture 2: Vote for Me—"I Want My Finger on the Button." (1:19)

Vote for me—I want my finger on the button.

I need a button. Give me a button.

Everyone should have their hand on the button. Not only North Korea and Iran but everyone. The democratization of nuclear weapons must be instituted forthright.

There can be no delay in freeing this indispensable tool from the dominion of a select elite and proliferating it into the hands of the individual. Some say, "A chicken in every pot"; how about, "A silo in every yard"? Protect yourself when you're out at school, shopping, or wherever your local conceal-and-carry lone-nut prowler may lurk with your very own nuclear deterrent. Protect yourself from foreign governments who want to entangle you in their quarrels. Protect yourself from your own unpredictable government. Pull the lever for the one who will put an effective deterrent in your hands. "Vote for me—I want my finger on the button."

Lecture 3: Autocriticism and the Legalization of Marijuana (2:45)

While we have ambitious plans for the forced re-education of broad segments of our society, our first step is reassessing our own values. As the radical avant-garde, we must now engage in what the communists used to call "autocriticism," a secular self-flagellation whereby we reassess our wrong-headed notions and attempt to reconcile dearly held beliefs with reality. This includes a sober look at what precipitated the situation we find ourselves in currently.

Just as with free speech, our generosity and permissiveness might have to be given more consideration.

I am speaking of course about the act of sharing and proliferating powerful and possibly dangerous substances such as rock 'n' roll, modernist art . . . and marijuana. The latter agent in particular being responsible for the schizophrenia, nihilism, and nonsense logic which are so chic at the moment.

In the immediate aftermath of the 2016 election, pundits fell over themselves to pound out theories of "What happened?" The answer, my friend, is blowing out of a dispensary in a major American city near you: it's called the legalization of marijuana.

The incessant smoking of reefer—a pastime that is essentially enforced—created the conditions for the current dark and incoherent political discourse. The paranoia triggered by today's high-octane "blowing," "dabbing," and "vaping" laid the groundwork for the modern conspiratorial social psychosis, with the results plain for all to see. The same pot smokers who improbably elected Obama in a euphoric, feel-good haze when their high was fresh have grown irritable, deranged, and depressed. They pull the lever in a psychotic funk of resentment on their way to buy a pint of Ben & Jerry's.

Marijuana's legalization in the USA, though in the works for decades, was a quick affair. Almost overnight, it seemed, more than half the states in the union suddenly passed laws legalizing marijuana either for medical or recreational use. Therefore, as per Bob Dylan's "Rainy Day Women #12 & 35" recommendation, much of the nation is now "stoned," most of the time.

Lecture 4: Autocriticism, Part II (2:42)

It seems irresponsible for Bob Dylan to insist that everybody must get stoned, but in his defense, the high, which he evangelizes on "Rainy Day Women #12 & 35," was from a different, less potent strain of the plant than is consumed today. It was also enjoyed by a different caste with values remote from the modern suburban user. It was an underground affectation, used by a subcultural elite of musicians, artists, mystics, and by an unrepresented underclass. Bob Dylan was only the most famous exponent of a scene of subterranean beatniks and poets who would smoke marijuana, write symbolist-inspired prose, and who were free of political affiliations beyond a perverse and unpredictable antiauthoritarianism. Though he marched for civil rights and wrote eloquent protest songs, Dylan was leery of organized politics or of being labeled one way or another. When he was presented with the prestigious Tom Paine Award alongside James Baldwin at a fancy liberal event in December of 1963, he insulted the audience and mumbled his empathy for Lee Harvey Oswald. In the immediate aftermath of the Kennedy assassination, this caused a wave of consternation.

Still, it was accepted that this beatnik crowd who smoked drugs were "artists," with a special relationship to a poetic truth beyond normal logic, and so Dylan's unconventional worldview was tolerated. While early incarnations of the folk music revival—such as the Pete Seeger's Weavers—were earnest, straightforward, humanist, and socialist, Dylan merged the highly popular and topical "folk" medium with the weed-soaked-paranoiac-introvert aesthetic of the beat poets. Dylan's perverse Tom Paine Award acceptance speech was a pot-fueled self-immolating nightmare event for both the recipient and the audience and was perhaps an eerie prophecy of the psychotic behavior which is quite normal now.

Lecture 5: Suburbanization of the Esoteric (2:33)
The Beatles' "invasion" of early 1964 marked the corporatization and suburbanization of the teen-

age urban rock 'n' roll phenomenon. Incandescent and new, they were irresistible at the time, even to cynics and sophisticates . . . such as Bob Dylan. Before the Beatles, most folkies disdained rock 'n' roll as teenybop bubblegum trash. Afterward, the folk crowd hung up their harmonicas and purchased amplifiers en masse. When the Beatles arrived in the USA, they hung out with all manners of stars, but their most auspicious meeting was with Bob Dylan, who introduced them to marijuana.

Instead of being assimilated into the star system of the day and taking their place alongside Dean Martin, Barbra Streisand, and 1964's other top stars, the Beatles were drawn to working-class music such as girl groups, R&B, country, and of course Bob Dylan. Their "invasion" was a blitzkrieg and they could have had anything they desired; residencies in Las Vegas, a string of films like Elvis, a live orchestra to accompany them. But as working-class bohemians, and under the new influence of marijuana, they retreated farther from mainstream show business to a fringe freak scene of London gallery owners, experimental filmmakers, pop artists, and orgy organizers.

Late-night marijuana sessions led them to sneakily adorn their records' sleeves with clues to their obsessions: winks and nods to other turned-on "heads" about what they were digging, whether it was Aleister Crowley, Karlheinz Stockhausen, Aubrey Beardsley, or Hinduism.

"All You Need Is Love" was their appropriation of the Buddhist teachings of the US Civil Rights Movement, nonviolence as extolled by Reverend Martin Luther King Jr., who radically proposed a sublime love to overcome the white-supremacist police state. A stoned revelation, "All You Need Is Love" became the anthem and ideology of what would be called the "hippie movement," the suburbanized version of the dropout "rambler" archetype from the folk-beat era. The Beatles' marijuana use led them farther out of show business to an ashram in India to meditate with a guru and eventually resulted in the mass alienation of fans due to the *Magical Mystery Tour* TV special—a stoned idea of Paul's based on the Merry Pranksters—and the subsequent alienation of the band from one another.

Lecture 6: Psychotic Reactionaries (2:51)

Meanwhile, fans, who had been explicitly instructed to smoke pot by the group—the most famous pop stars in the world with unimaginable sway over an enormous demographic—began, in a paranoid weed-induced frenzy, to deconstruct the very records they worshipped. The "Paul is dead" phenomena began, whereby the Beatles' signals to their illuminated peers about their interest in silent films and Satanism (a London art-scene fad in the mid-'60s) were discovered, dissected, and promulgated to be sinister clues in a dastardly plot of duplicity. Paul had been dead for years and the Beatles had cynically gone on with a replacement double . . . who had a penchant for show tunes! Psychotic pot smokers have now turned "Paul is dead" into an Internet industry which has become more sinister and deranged as THC levels in marijuana have become more and more potent.

In the hands of humanist hippies, marijuana induced a penchant for free love, outdoor concerts, weaving and crochet, geodesic domes, and communes, but also bizarre intrigue and psychosis like the "Paul is dead" conspiracy. As the central tenet of hippie culture was the "love" ideology, the drug's effect was largely benign; but fed to America's misanthropic *South Park* libertarians, neocons, neoliberals, gun freaks, video game champions, and football fans, legal suburban marijuana has begotten "pizza-gate," Russia-gate, and nuclear nihilism typified by confrontation with North Korea and Russia-hating mass hysteria.

In this context, the irresponsibility of Dylan's "Everybody Must Get Stoned" exhortation is boggling.

Lecture 7: Censorship Now!! *Reprise (2:20)*

Do you want to free yourself from the noise pollution of free speech and the dire consequences of its evil off-the-leash rampage? Well, my book *Censorship Now!!* will explain to you why A) free speech is a lie, and why B) it must be proscribed until *REEDUCATION* can be instituted or until we can institute a new regimen of what constitutes freedom of speech. This book, which washes the foul stigma off the word *censorship,* will tell you everything you need to know to defend its highly controversial opinions, which will be held by none of: your family, your friends, the public figures you have been taught to admire, the post-Enlightenment "thinkers" who have informed modern capitalist ideology.

It might be scary at first but this slim volume, colored green and black, with fourteen illustration collages by the author, will steel your resolve to stand firm in defending its apparently perverse promulgations which fly in the face of conventional thinking and the arrayed forces defending freedom of speech, such as:

The Gambino crime family
The Navy SEALs
T-Mobile
The Vanguard Group
Infinity Development Group
Opus Dei
The National Football Association
Raytheon
ExxonMobil
Bristol Myers Squibb
Citizens Council
Office of Naval Intelligence

Lecture 8: The Need for Cloud Reform
(Instrumental) (3:52)

Audience: [Sustained applause.]

FIN

PART IV

ALPHABET REFORM

Manifesto of the People's Provisional Army for Alphabet Reform

19

MANIFESTO OF THE PEOPLE'S PROVISIONAL ARMY FOR ALPHABET REFORM

QUESTION: Why can't words express the sublime?

QUESTION: Why are we confounded by our inability to communicate the "inexpressible"?

QUESTION: Why do we find ourselves at a "loss for words"—stymied by the insufficiency of language?

QUESTION: Why does humanity retreat so often into an anti-intellectual abandon of hard narcotics, kinky perversion, religious cults, violent crime, and dissonant rock 'n' roll?

QUESTION: Why does the globe reel from humanity's insatiable tendency toward viciousness, greed, callousness, and destruction?

ANSWER: The alphabet.

The alphabet. Twenty-six letters, a rogues' gallery of desultory, contrived devices, arbitrary and idiotic, each one representing a particular sound, each intended to be singular and indispensable. Every letter—though intended as conspicuous—is meant to be utilized in endless variations with other letters to form different words.

A clever idea, certainly, and one that was perhaps modern in its time, but like the corporate landscape we endure and the TV dinners we consume, the alphabet has outlived its usefulness and indeed can now be recognized as the principal root of the ills which plague the earth.

Why? Because the alphabet, intentionally compact to ensure mobility, is simply insufficient. The paucity of its letter forms means the sounds we are able to emit are constrained, as are the words we can build, and the things we can do, dream, and imagine. The alphabet as we know it has annihilated what could be words, sounds, expression, communication. Our emaciated vocabulary has not only starved our speech but also our imagination; our ability to transcend ancient models of tribalism, authoritarianism, social roles, and bogus moralities. The alphabet was invented during the time of the Caesars: an era of slavery, imperial brutality, fascist caprice, and cannibalistic class terror. No wonder our world is so twisted—we teach and are taught through the tool set of tyrants, despots, and zanies. When we paint ourselves with the palette of Nero, Tiberius, and Caligula, can we expect the outcome to be different?

An Apollonian gewgaw, the alphabet as we know it is a functional thing. Built and designed with an architect's eye for order, sense, rigidity, and inflexibility, its designers created a useful tool which worked well for commerce, governance, and commanding a cohort. But they excised the gasps, pants, and pagan incantations of intuitive communication as those didn't easily fit into their bureaucratic framework. By doing so, they relegated love, pain, intuition, and the senses into a netherworld where they were discredited; treated as superstition, madness, and/or hysteria.

Thus, all sensory reactions are wordless, while materialist concerns can be expressed with ease. Only in our dreams are we freed of business lingo, sensory deprivation, and the general sadism of speech.

The structuralists who dreamed up the alphabet were afraid of these dark spaces and turned the most vital part of expression into nonlanguage in a cruel and arbitrary demarcation which has impoverished humankind's ability to express, explore, or even truly feel.

There are speeches, books, volumes of written pages and oratory; spoken word, poetry. Books on tape and talk radio; people gossiping, discussing talking points, and hosting interview shows. But all of them are in a state of expressive poverty, all of them idiotic, living in a staunch, uptight martinet's fantasy where everything makes logical sense while the elephant in the room is all that's unsaid: the clamor of madness unexpressed, impossible to express, the spectral spooks of what's become the "subconscious."

These nonwords are the language of love, fear, pain, and also dreams. Dreams, once the guideposts to humankind's ambitions and desires, are inaccessible to the modern person because the alphabet has rendered them strange, nonsensical, incomprehensible. The "word made flesh" was a font.

Who built the alphabet? Functionaries. Fascists. Priests and praetorians who understood that control of the basic element of language would give reign to the content of thought and communication. Crazies who desired that expression suffer the same fate as the rest of their domain: imprisoned, enthralled, chained, parceled, exploited, mined, eroded, exploded in nuclear tests, and flung through the air as dust. The sort of imperialists who demarcate the globe through treaties and monopolies of violence. Why is there a word such as "sublime," which means "beauty which is experienced but cannot be explained or put into words"? Because the alphabet is an impoverished abomination which must be reformed posthaste.

Unconditionally, the alphabet is a supremacist tool for regulating certain kinds of language and certain kinds of expression, for elevating some kinds of animals and some forms of expression, and subverting, undermining, and denigrating others.

It's a tribal and xenophobic phenomenon whereby those who are unlettered are savages; "barbarians."

Why was God's name unspeakable in the Old Testament? The ancients were warning us, with a symbolic alert, that language—as conveyed through an alphabet—was deeply flawed, insufficient.

We need to reconfigure the alphabet. Rend it, warp it, bend it to our needs. Demolish its hierarchy of some letters over others, some in front and some more prominent, and consider how this guides our speech and our thoughts. The alphabet needs to be rearranged. Changed. The alphabet needs to be reformed.

Alphabet reform now.

FIN

POSTSCRIPT

Finally, liberation.

What we all intuited has now been made clear and evident.

We shall stop reading and writing forthwith and posthaste.

AGAINST THE WRITTEN WORD *is the book to end all books.*

Congratulations!

I.F. Svenonius

ABOUT THE AUTHOR

There is no information about the author.

Notes

Notes

Notes